Moving Beyond H.E.R.E!

Vonekham Phanithavong-Guthrie

iUniverse, Inc.
New York   Bloomington

Moving Beyond H.E.R.E!

iUniverse books may be ordered through booksellers or by contacting:

iUniverse
1663 Liberty Drive
Bloomington, IN 47403
www.iuniverse.com
1-800-Authors (1-800-288-4677)

ISBN: 978-1-4502-1027-0 (pbk)
ISBN: 978-1-4502-1028-7 (ebk)

Printed in the United States of America

iUniverse rev. date: 5/19/10

Dedicated in loving memory of

Fr. Larry Penzes (2003)

Clairey Marin (2000)

&

Maureen "Moe" Donovan (2005)

Preface:

On one overcast autumn day, a woman stood by the window, looked up at the sky and searched for the sun amidst the gray cumbersome clouds. Her hair rested in waves against her bare back, her eyes sullen. She pulled the blind cord, began to turn, and slowly scuffed back towards her bed. Little did she realize a glimmer of the sun's rays was reflecting through the blind shaft. Her eyes were focused in the wrong direction.

This scene captures the essence of the text you are about to read. I thank you for taking the time to read, reflect, and revive your life through the written word. Success is a word used to define achievement and drives the steps of most to do better, expect better, and anticipate more from the bounty we call life. Yet, only 5% of the population possesses 80% of the wealth in the United States. The question is why? How is it that of the thousands of college applicants that prepare, write, rewrite, hope and dream of becoming part of the elite and prestigious Ivy League club, only several thousand are accepted? Is it because the application pool of the few is so overwhelmingly phenomenal that the admissions officers can only accept those few? What breaks the decision barrier? The answer is self-motivation, self-presence, self-drive, self-perseverance, self-persistence, self-worth, and self-dedication.

College admissions officers make the difficult decision because of limits in enrollment numbers through the process of face-to-face interview. Just as employers do - post college. I know because I was in the nerve-racking position of being interviewed back in 1999. The meeting was scheduled for 10 a.m. on a cool spring day. I wore a light coat with pockets. My hands were in my pockets to hide my nervousness. A tall woman in a business suit approached with her hand outstretched. I quickly pulled my hand out from my pocket and dropped my keys on the floor.

The admissions officer looked at me, smiled, bent down, picked up the keys. "Nervous? Its okay, I don't bite," she said as she handed me my keys.

That little statement came over me like a wave of relief. It was then that something clicked and I realized the meeting was my opportunity to move beyond H.E.R.E. It was a moment in my life when I had to choose to stay where I was or to move where I was destined to go. It was my choice, my moment.

As I rose from my chair, I extended my open hand and took hold of the keys, placed them back in my pocket, smiled, extended my hand again, received her hand, shook firmly, looked her square in the eyes and said, "Thank you, I am so very humbled to be here today and have this opportunity to meet you."

She smiled and motioned for me to follow her to her office. We spoke for what seemed like hours, laughed and discussed the essay on my application. She commented how it really stuck out in her mind because I did not describe some major award-winning tournament as my greatest accomplishment but rather the challenges I overcame to access my education.

Each of us has the ability within us to be a shining star. It's the way in which we choose to shine that determines how bright our light will be. Those that shine the brightest are those that understand that their light reflects a stronger brilliance when shining through the glass than when shining in front of the glass. This concept will be explained in further detail during the course of the book.

These eight principles are not easily had nor do they provide the magic wand that will provide you a safe, smooth cruise through life. The chapters of this book and the lessons contained within them are derivatives of the experiences I've been fortunate enough to take part in or that have been shared by others; the failures you would own up to and learned from; the discoveries you would never give back; the joy that you are grateful for; the tears that made you stronger; the pain that tested your character; the doubt that you allowed to bind you; the vision that was laid before you; the purpose that has been set out for you and only you; and the journey that awaits you. Read these thoughts, stories, and the reflection exercises in its entirety and begin to move beyond your H.E.R.E! Some names and circumstances have been altered to protect individual privacy.

Chapter One: H.E.R.E!

What greater place to start than H.E.R.E. You're probably wondering what is H.E.R.E. Has this writer lost her mind? No, I promise you that is not the case. H.E.R.E is your present state of being, understanding, and knowledge. H.E.R.E are the feelings, experiences, persons or addictions that you allow to keep you and your gifts contained within you. It is a state we have all been victim to at some point and time in our life, myself included. H.E.R.E is the basketball coach that told you at the age of 10 that you didn't have what it takes to play competitively. If Michael Jordan had listened to that, we would not have had the opportunity to see him fly on the basketball court. It's holding onto the love that has already let go of you through memories, pictures, songs, and places. It's not going to church because you feel unappreciated. It's ending a friendship over something as menial as cost of a broken pair of glasses. It's rehashing old wounds by throwing them into an argument with the one you claim to love. It's blaming others for your own shortcomings. It's expectation without preparation. It's being brilliant but keeping the brilliance to yourself. It's wishing something better would come along but never taking the steps to seek it out. It's not exploring beyond your own perceptions. It's allowing differences to separate you instead of enhance you. H.E.R.E can mean so many things to so many people, but for this writer H.E.R.E means <u>H</u>indrances <u>E</u>ndanger <u>R</u>easonable <u>E</u>levation.

Hindrances are a present or past circumstance that you continue to give life to, allowing it to stall your personal and/ or professional progress. If your progress is being stalled, you are not only **endanger**ing your own development, but also the development of those that will come after you. We never truly realize our influence over others until we let them down. As a leader, no matter the capacity in business, church or the community, our actions have a greater impact, much more than our bottom line. It affects all those employed, volunteering and witnessing the action taking place at some level - conscious or subconscious. Growth is a process. One cannot begin as an assistant and be promoted to CEO overnight. **Reasonable** reminds us that we need to assess the goals we are striving for, take a realistic review of our ability to make a substantial contribution to a project and then put into place the steps to attain that goal. If I only know how to turn on the computer, I should not be pursing the position of Vice President of Technology.

Elevation points to our greatest strength and weakness at the same time because we have to rely on the foundation we established. Yet, it places us in a vulnerable place where we rest on the foundation others have built for us. You often here the phrase, "standing on the shoulders of those who came before you," at inspirational keynote addresses. I know because I've used that phrase but it is such a true and relevant statement. If you work for an organization that has never had a female executive, the challenges you will face will be greater than for a woman in an organization where female leadership already exists. Anyone who has had the opportunity to be the trailblazer of a project, organization, etc. understands this far to well. Putting aside what is legally appropriate and politically correct, you are at some level being measured by the standard of your predecessor. Elevation is a wonderful accomplishment, but also brings with it an unwritten and often unspoken responsibilities.

The principles shared throughout this book will be demonstrated through story. In these chapters, the vignettes will show the ways others have been able to move from their H.E.R.E that kept them in emotional, mental, spiritual and sometimes physical bondage. The following interpretations are of some people I've been fortunate enough to know, learn from and grow from.

The Glass Half Full/ Half Empty

Reverend Sipkin was on a mission to bring young people to Christ. He had toured the globe, traveling from one small village to another, preaching of healing, acceptance and sacrifice. He entered the seminary soon after college, accepting a call from the Lord. His father left when he was 10 years old, and the only memories he had of him were images of his father in a drunken stupor. He recalled one distinct memory when his father controlled the gas and brake pedals of the car as he steered them safely home from the neighbors' card game six blocks away. Rev. Sipkin was a priest, a holy man. He eventually forgave his father one day. He prayed over many who were afflicted with alcoholism.

One morning, as he took his routine walk around the church grounds, Rev. Sipkin was mugged and brutally beaten. The thieves did not get much as all he had in his wallet was forty dollars. It took Rev. Sipkin months to recover. As he lay in the hospital bed, the pain was immense, but dulled with Morphine. He was soon discharged, but the pain medication did not fully relieve the aches. One afternoon as he sat in the living room and the pain consumed him. He looked over to the liquor cabinet and poured a small glass of brandy.

Months later that glass became a bottle a day but he kept it together and many did not know about his new practice. Soon he could no longer hide his addiction and the church had him admitted into a rehabilitation center, which became a revolving door for the next 10 years of his life. He became bitter. The anger that he thought he had let go of towards his father surfaced in therapy.

Then, one day a man approached Rev. Sipkin as he sat in the parlor and said, "If a man of the cloth can't escape this addiction. I'm certain there is no hope for me."

Rev. Sipkin looked at him. Stunned at first, looked up to heaven, took hold of the man's hands, recited a quick prayer, smiled and walked away. Rev. Sipkin began to pray with a fervor like never before in his hospital room for three days.

He picked up the phone and began making calls in search of his father. Weeks later he found out that his father only lived three miles from his rehab center. Rev. Sipkin asked his sister to drive him to his father's house. She did it, but with great reluctance. As they approached the house, Rev. Sipkin began to perspire and his hands began to shake. He sat in the car for sometime just staring at the wooden door. He said a quick "Our Father" opened the car door and rang the bell. An old woman answered the door.

Her clothes were tattered, and she had on a red apron that was covered in oil stains. "Father, can I help you?" she asked.

It wasn't until that moment that he realized he was wearing his collar.

He cleared his throat. "Hmmm, yes. I'm looking for Ronald Sipkin."

Panicked the woman inquired, "Has something happened?"

"Yes, I mean no. I simply need to have a word with him."

Soon after a man approached the door, his stomach extended over his waistband wearing a white t-shirt. Rev. Sipkin watched as he made his way to the door and noticed the paleness of his face, the way one side of his face dropped a little more than the other and the sloth of his walk.

"Who are you? What ya want?" He snapped.

"I'm Rev. Sipkin."

The man stood still for a moment, speechless before blurting out, "I ain't got no money for you, you grown now. What ya want?"

Rev Sipkin squeezed the rosary beads in his pocket tightly and said softly, "I forgive you with the love of the Lord." He turned and walked away. The wind hit the back of his neck as the door slammed behind him.

When Rev. Sipkin returned to the car, he began to weep. His sister held his hand, hugged him. "We deserve better than that as a father," she said pointing her finger toward the door.

Rev Sipkin looked up, "We already have better... the Lord. I pray for mercy on our natural father's soul."

Rev. Sipkin returned to the pulpit about a month later and shared a sermon on his redemption. The prayer line that morning extended to the back of the church. He shared his testimony with the congregation to help others heal. He continues to minister to this day, a blessed man of the Lord.

One Must Fall to Stand

For a moment during the graduation service at Columbia University I self-actualized and then was consumed with the misguided notion that it was all about me. The humility that allowed me to survive the rigor and demands of academia, motherhood, work and being a wife were pushed aside with arrogance and a bloated ego. Sometimes I wonder how I even fit through the doors of Lerner Hall that day. I refused, in reflection, wonderful career opportunities.

My attitude was the company needs me, don't they know who I am? I soon learned not so much. And six months post graduation, I found myself unemployed with debt overwhelming me. I graduated Columbia with a Platinum American Express and then, had just barely enough to put food on the table. I turned down another job for a company located just three blocks of the Twin Towers. The following week September 11th happened. I recall watching the newsreel of the planes as they struck each tower. At the time, my husband was working overseas on a training tour in India. Everyone was in a panic that day. I did not speak with my husband until the next morning. The U.S. Embassy and his employer had placed him in a safe house and a month passed before he was allowed to return to the United States.

About a month later, I humbled myself and convinced a medical billing firm to hire me, making less than I had earned out of high school, but it was work. It was during my time there, about six months, I learned about the intricacies of the medical industry. The CEO soon saw my abilities and had me work closely with his two account managers setting up their presentation materials and conducting the review of research. He even gave me the task of figuring out the formula to measure lost revenue for Medicaid and I figured it out. If I only had that formula now? It made the firm millions, but I soon began to send out resumes with a focus toward the medical industry. I was caught in a rock and a hard place. Employers identified me as either over-qualified or under-qualified.

One morning just as I began to settle into my day, I received an intercom call that I had an emergency phone call. I picked up the phone to the frantic voice of my mother on the other end.

She kept shouting, "He's been shot; he's been shot." over and over again.

It took about 5 minutes to calm her down enough to ask who's been shot.

She began shouting again, "Larry, Larry. Come home, hospital, come home!"

"Wait, wait. Shot where, how?" I shouted back. The women in my office began to congregate around my cubicle.

She shouted back, "Come home, come home, he's been shot."

I hung up the phone and headed immediately toward the CEO's office.

He looked up as I entered the doorway and said, "Is everything okay?"

"No, my Godfather's been shot."

He stood up from his chair, "Are you going to be okay to drive?"

"Yeah, I'm sure it's no big deal. He's a Lieutenant Colonel in the Air Force. He's trained for this type of stuff. They probably only got him in his leg or something."

The CEO looked at me strangely. "You sure?"

"Yeah, I'm good." At the time it sounded good, just a leg wound, no big deal.

I gathered my things and headed to my car. It was then that I realized what if it's not a leg wound, what if it's more serious than that. I sat in my car for a few moments and wept, wiped my tears and went into *it's time to be the strong one* mode. This was my typical role during times of tragedy and confusion in my family.

When I arrived to my mother's home, she was frantic – walking back and forth between the bathroom and her bedroom. I sat on the living room couch for a few minutes to take it all in before turning on the television in her bedroom. I quickly changed the channel, manually, to Channel 12 News. On the scrolling news bar it read "breaking story – Long Island priest shot." The same line scrolled past the screen over and over and over and over.

"Mom, you about ready?" I asked.

"Why are you so calm?" she huffed.

"Let's find out how bad he is before we lose it," I replied. She stared me down for a few moments and then went back into the bathroom again.

I knocked on the door. "Come on, let's go to the hospital. He must be at Mercy," I said.

The door quickly flew open. "Yeah, he's there. We have to go to St. Frances first to get Connie," she replied and then closed the door.

"Why?" I asked confused by her statement.

"She wants to come with us to the hospital," she shouted through the door.

"Who cares, she's not family. We're wasting time, let's go." I hollered back.

The door flew open and my mother was finally dressed - face and clothes. With tears in her eyes and a crackling voice she said firmly, "We're picking up Connie."

"Fine! I'm going outside to pull the car up-front. Come out when you're ready."

My nerves were beginning to get the best of me as I sat waiting in the car. My leg was shaking and I began thinking of the worse case scenario. *What if he's dead, what if he's dead. No, no can't think that way.*

Before long my mother flew into the car. We drove to St. Frances without uttering a word. The radio played, but I can't recall what songs. I pulled the car in a parking spot in the rear of the rectory by the kitchen entrance way and waited in the car as my mother jumped out to get Connie. The door opened and the pastor came out. He leaned over to tell my mother something. She collapsed in his arms. I knew exactly what he told her – My Godfather was dead. He waved at me to come in. My behavior was almost robotic - turned off the car, opened the door and walked up the cement steps, but I felt nothing. When I walked into the eating area of the kitchen, my mother was sobbing surrounded by a host of people comforting her and rubbing her back. The pastor closed the door behind me.

He hugged me and said, "I'm so sorry." I cringed a little and then gently pushed him back. "I didn't want you to hear from the media. That's why we asked you to come here first."

I looked at him, smiled and asked, "Where is the telephone? I have to call the rest of the family."

He directed me to a nearby office. He touched my arm and asked, "Are you okay?"

"Yeah. I have to be."

I called my husband who had been following the story on the news and told him to get the children from school. I was going to be awhile. His immediate reaction was I'm going to Lynbrook to kill the murderer. After about 20 minutes, he calmed down. I called my father who began sobbing immediately. I listened for a while and then I told him I had to go and would be home soon. I called my sisters in Florida. They both began sobbing. I listened for a while and then told them to come home to New York.

After I hung up the phone, tears began to well up but I took a deep breath and did not let them escape from my eyes. I got up from the chair and went to check on my mother. She had calmed down a bit and was ready to go home. The few parishioners and friends of my mother who were present then shifted their attention to me. They came toward me with open arms to embrace me.

I stepped back, held my hand up, palm facing outward and said, "I'm good."

A longtime friend of my Godfather's and my mother's work colleague, Connie, looked at me as if something was wrong with me. Her eyes were red. I leaned against the radiator and waited. About a half hour passed before my mother was calm enough to get into the car. We thanked everyone and went home in silence.

The experience at the wake and funeral and the mourning process is something I'll reserve to discuss in another section of this book. In summary, it was an experience unlike I had ever experienced then and now. He died in March, about a month after we surprised him with a lavish 50th birthday party complete with a "Let's go Jets" theme. The media focused on me for some reason. My family and I were on newspaper covers whether we liked it or not. It's funny when my Godfather made the decision as a young priest to save a refugee family impacted by the Vietnam War, he chose us. He brought us to America and made sure we had shelter, food and a catholic school education. The first time he took us to Jones beach, shortly after we arrived on Long Island, the story was hidden in the pages of the paper. He cut it out and framed it. Now, his murder was on the front page and embedded all through the papers as the reporters relentlessly analyzed the event sadly hoping for controversy that simply did not exist. A genuinely good person was a new and hard-to-swallow concept for the media, it seemed.

About two weeks later, I received a call from a place called Transitions. Evidently, I had applied for a job there back in February. At the time I couldn't recall too much. The woman on the line asked me to come in for an interview. I accepted the invitation.

The morning of the interview, I had an indifferent feeling. In the past I would have been rehearsing my interview nervously in my mind over and over as I drove to the interview site. As we spoke, the manager shared with me that she was not planning to call me in for an interview because I was over qualified, but when she saw me in Newsday she thought she'd see if I might be interested in joining her team. I made it to the final round of interviews and met with the Executive Director. We talked about my Godfather most of that interview, and I shared with her that he would have probably been in a rehab center much like the one I was interviewing for, if he had survived. We shook hands and I waited for "the call."

Some weeks later, I was offered the position and was provided a higher salary than posted. During my time at Transitions there were moments of great accomplishment and moments of frustration, but working with the patients and watching them heal and develop was the therapy I needed to get me through the first stage of my healing process, though at the time I didn't realize it. I was able to stand tall on my own two feet for the first time in almost a year since graduating college.

Church Hurt

When one first learns of God and feels his presence, the world is an exciting place as the Bible takes on life. The desire to learn and take part in ministry is overwhelming. Some step into action before they are personally or spiritually ready for the challenges along the way. People that work in churches, just like organizations, at the end of the day, are people with their own personalities, quirks, and their own H.E.R.E. Melody was newly saved and excited about learning about Jesus. She plugged in attending Bible study on Wednesday evening, Sunday service and Sunday school at Greater Faith Temple. She approached the pastor, shared with him her gift, which was her singing voice, and her experience in the music industry. He quickly referred her to the Choir Director and positioned her as the Assistant Director.

The other 30 members of the choir were nearly not as excited by her appointment as she was. After all, she was a new member and some of the choir members had been in the church over 20 years. Melody's position was announced at the leadership meeting. She sat around the table and observed some friendly faces and some cold hard stares. Taken aback, Melody left the meeting confused and uncertain about whether she should have gotten involved. Another meeting commenced the following month and Melody had been asked to identify some research about a few new songs that would aid in ushering in the spirit and setting the tone for the service.

Prior to coming to the meeting, Melody emailed her selections and a write up about her reasoning for choosing certain songs. At the point in the meeting where song selection was being discussed, none of the other leaders mentioned her email or document. Melody raised her hand and the pastor acknowledged her.

"Did any of you have the opportunity to review my email?" she asked.

The pastor looked around the table, a few minutes passed and no one replied.

Suddenly, Deacon Neuman stood up and said, "The selections were terrible. You don't know what you're talking about."

Shocked and angry, Melody sat frozen and it took her a few moments and deep breaths before she leaned forward to give her response.

Before she was able to utter a word the pastor chimed in. "Deacon, you will treat everyone at this table with respect. I brought Melody here. She has experience and wisdom we can learn and grow from."

He looked toward Melody, smiled and nodded.

"Well," she swallowed hard, "had you read through the email and reviewed the document you would have seen that I only recommended three of the eight songs on the list and identified my reasoning for those selections. I'm not expecting everyone to agree with my opinion but we should all keep an open mind and have a discussion."

The meeting was soon adjourned and Melody returned home contemplating resigning from her newly appointed position. Later that day, three of the church leaders including Deacon Neuman emailed apologies to Melody.

Melody stayed on as Assistant Choir Director for four years. Overtime, she grew despondent over how the leaders operated and made decisions. Melody would make a recommendation and it would fall on deaf ears. The church was beginning to become stagnant. She walked away from the church in anger, hurt and frustration. Weeks passed, then months but Melody knew she had to forgive before she could return to the church. She had to be able to see those that had hurt her without thinking hurtful thoughts. She had to mature in her faith.

Eight months later, she decided one morning to go back to Greater Faith Temple. The number of members who embraced her when service ended overwhelmed her. After service she went to the common fellowship area.

The pastor saw her and gave her a big bear hug, "Missed you girl, where you been?" and then quickly walked back into his office.

A few moments later, the pastor's wife grabbed Melody by the hand and led her to her office. Once the door was closed, she embraced her.

"What's going on? Where have you been?"

Melody's eyes welled up and she began to breakdown. "I've missed you and pastor so much. I thought you didn't want me here so I left."

The pastor's wife's eyes also welled up. "Baby, never think that. We love you. Don't allow others to cloud that. We need you more than ever. You have a purpose here and I need for you to stand in the gap as we go through this transition time. You have the expertise and wisdom that God only gave you." Melody nodded.

The two embraced and the pastor's wife urged Melody to speak directly with the pastor about what happened. In the coming weeks Melody came face to face with those that had injured her. She hugged them both, smiled and thanked God in her heart for allowing her to grow to that point.

Marriage of Convenience

Four years passed, the purchase of a home, the purchase of a car, the birth of a child and yet, the wedding ring was still absent from Tammy's finger. She knew that she loved Shawn, but the last time they walked past the diamond ring section of the jewelry store he hyperventilated. The days rolled by and one afternoon as they sat at the dinner table with Tammy's parents, her elderly father spoke of his hope to see all of his daughters married and cared for before his passing, something passed over Shawn's face. As they drove home limited words were exchanged. The next morning as they sat for breakfast Shawn asked Tammy if she wanted to get married.

Without hesitation Tammy responded, "Yes!" They hugged for several minutes. Shawn kissed the baby on his head, took a moment to look at his family and then left for work.

The announcement was made to the family. Some celebrated while others wondered.

Tammy plunged head first into the wedding plans. She oversaw every detail and Shawn was happy to let her take the lead. Before long the wedding day arrived. Tammy was saddened because her sister could not attend the event due to health restrictions and she called on a friend to step into the role of matron of honor. Little did she know it was because her sister was not convinced the marriage was occurring for the right reasons. When she spoke with Tammy about that reason for getting married, Tammy simple said it was time. Her sister urged her to postpone the wedding and to think seriously about what it meant to be married.

Tammy angered by her sister's request said, "Not everyone can have a perfect marriage like you."

Her sister retorted, "There is no such thing. Marriage is work, rooted in love and a covenant set before God. Do you realize what that means? You're making a promise before God."

"Let's drop it." Tammy sighed.

Tammy made a beautiful bride on a cool spring morning. The wedding pictures made their display on Shutterfly, the presents were opened, checks deposited and the honeymoon was taken.

Six months went by and Tammy was in her living room one day frantically looking for a bracelet she had worn her entire adult life. It was given to her by her first love but she would never tell Shawn that. Times got rough. Tammy became ill and couldn't work. Shawn took on two jobs to pay the mortgage at the cost of being with his family. Tammy began to get lonely. She focused on her appearance thinking if she lost some weight her health issues would dissipate, her low self-esteem would change and she would feel better about herself. She was wrong.

Shawn did not even see her slip away. She took comfort in another man's arms and before long the secret came out. Remarkably, Shawn was understanding and blamed himself for the breakdown in their relationship and feverishly sought to reconcile. When Tammy confessed her affair. He then shared that he too had been unfaithful prior to their marriage, shortly after their son was born. Tammy held onto his confession and felt that it confirmed her actions were validated. The baby was now 3 years old.

Tammy called her sister, her voice a quiver. "You were right."

"I wasn't trying to be right. I was trying to protect you from yourself."

"What do I do now?" Tammy asked.

"Pray and do what your heart leads you to do. Think about the baby and then think about you and your husband. I love you and I'll be praying too," her sister responded.

Tammy and Shawn separated a year and four months after they walked down the aisle.

Just understanding your H.E.R.E circumstance is half the battle. The experiences and processes shared were not easy by any stretch of the imagination. Strength comes in learning and growing. Many people already know what their H.E.R.E is, yet, they continue to give one-time life events life and allow them to consume their present joy. Addiction, loss, and hurt are all very real and powerful emotions. They bind many people to live lives where they cannot see the light that follows behind and shines before them. They are looking in a direction that only leads to darkness, which is a frightening and lonely place.

Coming to a place in your life when you can acknowledge your H.E.R.E and take the actions to move beyond it will only occur when you take the steps towards personal development through reflection, prayer, forgiveness, and gratefulness. Every person finds the path that works best for him or her whether it is reading inspirational stories, having a life changing event or developing a true relationship with the Lord. It all begins with a very key and important step - coming to the realization that H.E.R.E exists, wanting to move beyond it and making the choice to take the steps to make that happen.

Chapter 2: Mirror, Mirror

In Walt Disney's classic first princess feature film "Snow White and the Seven Dwarfs" the evil stepmother performs a daily ritual of looking into her magic mirror but never seeing her true reflection. She utters, "Mirror, mirror on the wall who's the fairest of them all" and the mirror affirms her beauty until, that is, Snow White became of adult age. This film captured the themes of good and bad, selflessness and selfishness, insecurity and confidence and the power of love. These are some of the common themes of life. It drives our society in many ways. The ritual performed by the evil stepmother mirrors many individuals daily mental struggle with self-love. We look into the mirror and begin to see physical flaws, dissecting those sections of our body, face, hair that could be improved. It's the reason the beauty industry remains one of the most lucrative industries as we search for real beauty. I contest that the beauty already exists and it's the lens of life that we use that cloud our vision.

Envision the first time you held your newborn child, your niece or nephew, and remember the pure beauty that lay in your arms in need of your support, protection, and love. There are few that would disagree with me that a baby is beautiful. They see through the eyes of hope, love, and expectation. Yet, as the years pass, as age advances, and as life knocks them down, that vision becomes tainted by disappointment, hurt, fear and helplessness. Why is it that an act as simple as getting up and walking forward can be as painful as a broken limb or worse a broken heart? A mirror only reflects back what our eyes perceive. Every blemish, every scare has a memory, a story connected to it.

Taking Flight

In 1977, the Vietnam War was no longer in the headlines and the American army, for the most part, had left Southeast Asia. Laos was now occupied by the Communist regime and those that supported the Royals were being purged. A young mother of three little girls became a widow, head of her house, and prisoner in her own country all in the same month. As the months passed and she witnessed daily searches of her home, the woman realized she had to do something. In the market there was talk about a man that could help you escape the country. He had no name and was only referred to as "the boatman" but the cost for the guide across the Mekong River was hefty.

The young mother began to sell what items of value she had left in her home. She found some of the money her husband had stored in the beds of their children. She carved slits in the trunk of the banana trees in her backyard and hid the money there. She also hid money in banana peels in the garbage. After a few months she had saved enough to pay for the boatman's assistance. The marketplace was busy as many prepared for the festival of lights that coming week. The young mother prepared for her escape. The boatman's handlers placed five sleeping pills, a map, and instructions wrapped in a banana leaf in the young mother's hand.

Later that evening, the young mother took her three daughters to her parents' home in the country for a feast for the festival of lights and the Buddha's blessings. The young mother held her mother a little longer and tighter than before that evening. She could not tell her about the planned escape or her entire family would be killed. When the young mother returned home she prepared her daughters' evening snack. She mashed up the sleeping pills and mixed it into her 2-year-old's soup and mixed it into her 6-month-old's bottle. Once the younger daughters were fast asleep, she woke her 9 year old and explained to her what was to happen and the she would have to carry her baby sister into the woods and follow the man to the limestone waterfalls. The oldest daughter held her mother and cried quietly.

When they reached the first meeting point, the mother and her eldest daughter had to leave the two younger daughters in the trust of strangers and make their way to the riverbank. Some ten minutes later, the eldest daughter was helped into a small fishing boat as the mother slowly moved into the water. They both waited and before long they saw small bodies being thrown from the cliff to the boatman below. Soon enough the young mother and eldest daughter realized it was the babies. One child struck the edge of the boat, but was caught before she hit the water and placed into the boat. The young mother cringed and began to cry when she realized it was her youngest child.

The journey began across the river. Three boats were making their way across the water that evening. About a quarter of the way to the midpoint in the river, a child screamed in fear and gunfire blared. Bullets hit the river from all directions, shouting and alarms could be heard. Luckily, the boat with the children and the boat that the young mother swam along side, were closer to the safe point in the Mekong River. The eldest daughter placed her hand over her mouth as tears fell from her eyes and she watched the other boat get riveted by bullets and sink into the water. Physically and emotionally exhausted, the young mother collapsed on the riverbank in Thailand.

She was awoken by the voices of Thai policemen who were pacing around her. She quickly ran to her children. Her baby was bleeding from her head and non-responsive. She pleaded with the policemen to let her take the child but they insisted she was dead. Her persistence and the empathy of the police chief allowed her to take her baby with her to the Thai jail cell. Some hours later the baby awoke.

That young mother and her daughters would spend the next 2 years in a refugee camp surviving on a daily food ration of one hard boiled egg and a small coffee cup serving of white rice. The young mother often went without food and watched as her daughters' bellies began to swell. She cried at night and prayed for her daughters' lives. Eventually, the young mother and her daughters were sponsored by a Catholic church on Long Island, NY and were brought to America.

Her hope was answered in the form of a young priest that rallied to take on this missionary work. Her youngest daughter suffered no brain damage, nor was she slow in her mental processes. She went on to graduate at the top of her class from Columbia University in New York City. To this day she carries a scar on her forehead that reminds her of the ordeal she survived before she could even talk or walk.

A Prophecy Confirmed

David and Leslie were a young couple. They had three children and were content with the size of their family. One evening in October, the husband was feeling a little romantic and a month later a home pregnancy test revealed that baby number four was on its way. The couple had limited means and were not financially ready to welcome a fourth child. They soon came to terms with their new situation and prayed that God would make a way.

Leslie was beginning to feel pregnant and the day before her five-month checkup David was laid off from work. On the way to the doctor he was yelling into his cell phone with his former employer. As they sat in the waiting room, David was distracted and murmuring as he flipped through the waiting room magazines. His phone rang just as Leslie was called into the office. He motioned for her to go in and he'd soon follow, as he walked into the hallway. The office visit was routine at best, pee in a cup, get on the scale, etc. Finally, Doctor Ross came into the room.

He said, "Let's take a look and see what you created this time." As he turned on the sonogram machine, he hummed as he usually did while he poured on the ice cold lotion and began moving around the hand wand. The static and swoosh of the machine was very familiar and Leslie was very confident in Dr. Ross. He had saved her son.

He turned the monitor so Leslie could see and said, "There's the head, feet..." and then he paused and turned his head for a moment. "I'm so sorry Leslie... the baby's heartbeat just stopped."

With a confused expression Leslie looked at Dr. Ross and said, "What do you mean?"

He repeated, "The baby's heartbeat just stopped, I'm so sorry sweetie." He gave her a few moments to collect her emotions.

"Okay, now what?" she responded.

Dr. Ross gave her an odd look, wiped her belly, covered it with a sheet and moved his chair closer to her head.

He held her hand and said, "It'll be okay but we need to schedule surgery. The baby is too big for you to pass on your own. The pain will be unbearable. I'll get the earliest appointment I can for a D & C. The girls will call you. If it becomes unbearable before that date call me and we'll push you in through emergency... okay?"

He smiled. Leslie nodded as the tears welled up in her eyes.

David was just entering into the waiting area as Leslie walked out of the office area.

"What happened? Are you and the baby okay?" asked David.

"Let's go home. I'll tell you in the car." He grabbed Leslie's jacket and wrapped it around her shoulders. He opened her door and closed it behind her and then jumped into his side of the car before noticing the trail of tears on Leslie's face.

"What happened?" he asked as he grabbed her hand.

"The baby is gone."

"What do you mean the baby's gone?" he was puzzled.

"In the office, the baby..." Leslie began to sob. "The baby's heart stopped. I have to have surgery in two weeks to have the baby removed. Dr. Ross said it would be too painful to pass on my own." David sat in the car and did not respond. He turned on the engine and began driving.

Before long he became angry and then began to tear up. He dialed his former employer and yelled at him through the phone shouting, "The stress you caused my wife has killed my baby."

The days rolled by, and Leslie stayed in bed. The pain left her unable to walk. The date of the scheduled surgery came soon enough. This was the first major surgery Leslie ever had, the first where she would be asleep. She was scared as they wheeled her into a cold metal room. Strangers in masks and blue paper dresses were all around her. She kept looking around. Dr. Ross took off his mask and moved his chair toward her.

He held her hand as tears emerged from her eyes and said, "It's going to be okay. Start counting backwards from ten."

Leslie woke up in the recovery room. As she opened her eyes Dr. Ross and David were talking. She watched as they shook hands.

Dr. Ross rushed over to her bedside when he saw her gesture to move up. "Whoa now... give the anesthesia sometime to wear off. You'll be unsteady for a while and may vomit, but take your time and rest now. I have another patient. I'll see you in a few weeks. I gave David all the instructions." Dr. Ross shook her hand as he usually did and left.

Leslie hated being in the hospital and asked David to call for a wheelchair to leave. As the aid wheeled her out of the hospital she began to vomit. David rubbed her back for a few moments and then ran to get the car. He helped her into the passenger side seat, closed the door and drove home. When they arrived at the house, David carried Leslie into their room, placed her in bed and let her sleep. It was the week before Easter.

David's mother came over later that day and cooked dinner for the family. Leslie's mother could not fly out to be with her until the following week. Leslie stayed in bed, crying and sleeping. Easter morning, David dressed the children for church and got himself together. Leslie crawled to their closet and pulled down a dress.

David came out of the bathroom and stood over her, "Have you lost your mind?"

"I need to go to church. I need help with this David." Leslie began to sob again.

"That's not happening, get healthy first. We'll get through this." He picked her up and placed her back in bed.

Leslie folded her arms and huffed, "I'm going to church."

David called for his mother-in-law, "Please talk some sense into your daughter."

Leslie's mom sat next to her in the bed and held her as David and the children left for church. Later that day Leslie crawled out of her bed and began to pray. She questioned God as to why he took her child. Thanked him for her family and prayed feverishly for the hurt to go away. Three weeks later Leslie returned to church. The Bishop of the church called her to the altar that service for prayer. As she walked to the center of the church, she began to cry. The Bishop began to pray and like a bolt of lightening Leslie fell forward onto the floor.

The Bishop called out, "You're work is not done. God sees you. You need no one's affirmation but the Lord's. He affirms you in the name of Jesus Christ. A seventh door has been opened unto you." He began to instruct the congregation to pray. This continued on for about 10 minutes before Leslie was helped to her feet.

The Bishop hugged her in his teddy bear way, wiped her tears and whispered in her ear, "Your work is not done, it's yet to begin. You have a high anointing on your life... woman of faith. Walk in your divine call."

Leslie thought she was being punished but realized that she was being developed for greater ministry. She now works with challenged youth in leadership at her church.

I Am the Wife

Stephanie married Walter right out of community college. They both had great ambition, but life got in the way. Days became routine, almost monotonous. They had their two children, one boy and one girl. Their life was complete or so they thought. When Walter's mother became very ill and was placed on dialysis the responsibility and time weighed heavy on Walter's heart and his daily schedule. Stephanie was already not a fan of David's family that she perceived as blood sucking life drainers and her mother-in-law felt the same of her. The two had formed a workable relationship, at best, with moments of closeness along the way but ever so brief moments. Walter came home after midnight two nights a week to take his mother to dialysis treatments. His siblings were unreliable and often unpredictable.

This new time shift placed a heavy strain on their marriage. Before long they argued daily and Walter began to go out after dropping his mother off at home. At first, he'd stay out a few extra hours, which turned into the entire evening and after two years the entire weekend. Stephanie decided she needed to finish her Bachelors degree and began putting the steps in place to make that happen. Within six months, not only was she accepted into a program at the local state college, but she was also provided a full scholarship. She told Walter she was going back to school with or without his support. Walter agreed they'd work out the schedule but did so begrudgingly.

At night, Stephanie, would stare out her window and wait. She'd wait for the sun to rise, she'd wait to hear the first bird chirp and she'd wait for Walter to come home. He often stumbled into the house around 6 a.m. sometimes later and would want sex. There was a time when the smell of alcohol was a turn on for Stephanie but now it made her stomach turn. At first she'd give in to his request, but then realized she had no idea where he had been and began to resist. This angered Walter and he said it was her duty as his wife. She would struggle each time he'd come home for a little while, but eventually concede and during that time stare at the wall repeating in her mind *"I am the wife."*

On a cold February morning, Stephanie prayed that God would stop what was happening. She prayed for release from her marriage. She prayed his car would crash. She prayed for his deliverance. God would not release her and reminded her of the good that still rested in him. That next day she called her pastor and asked his counsel. He told her to stay still and listen to the voice of God. At the time, she didn't understand what that meant. Three months later, her mother-in-law passed suddenly. Stephanie was the first one at the hospital and the last one to speak with her before she slipped into a coma.

A week passed before the decision was made to pull the plug. She took her last breath four hours later. Walter was devastated. He laid in bed for two days and wept. The funeral was ornate and well attended. The preacher made a call for salvation and forgiveness. Walter continued to booze even more now to numb the pain. Stephanie had had enough and one morning when he returned home his clothes were stuffed in a garbage bag and placed on the steps with a note that read *"Get out!"* He became so enraged that he ran upstairs and began to choke and slap her. Stephanie fought back and dug her nails into his hands. He released his grip and she ran into her daughter's bedroom and locked the door. She sat in the corner by the window sobbing. After 20 minutes of banging on the door and cussing, Walter left.

Stephanie called the police and for the first time she spoke about the abuse. She realized as she spoke that every time he pushed her, manhandled her, forced himself on her, that he was no longer treating her as his wife. All the emotions came to a head and she was overwhelmed with grief. She knew better. How could she allow this to happen? The officer advised her of her options and gave her some pamphlets where she could get some counseling. The following day she filed a petition for an order of protection and legal separation at the family court.

Three months passed and the anger between Walter and Stephanie had subsided. They began to discuss the next steps – divorce or reconciliation.

Walter had hoped he'd get another chance and had begun to get help for his drinking. He even confessed to Stephanie that he also was doing cocaine. She just couldn't believe it and told him she'd pray that God helps him with his addictions. Six more months passed. Stephanie and Walter spent Sundays together with the children but still lived in separate homes and one Sunday morning Walter gave his life to Christ. He never picked up another drink or snorted another line. Stephanie's prayers were answered. The pastor reminded her that if you wait on God look at the great things he can do. Stephanie and Walter now have a loving marriage based on mutual respect.

In each of these three vignettes, the injuries and scars these individuals had were the situations that developed them personally and spiritually. When you are going through such challenges seeing the lesson is never easy. True forgiveness and letting go is never easy. Each person had a mirror moment when they had to face the truth before them, make a decision and then cope with the consequences that came out of that choice.

Often simply making the choice is frightening but it must be done and not making a choice is a choice. If you don't choose someone will choose for you or worse the options will disappear all together. Don't be afraid when your mirror moment happens move toward it and then move pass it. Scars, internal or external, are reminders that you survived and were healed not that you're still injured. Proudly wear your battle scars!

Chapter 3: Mercy Mountains

Mountains are wondrous and mysterious masses of land. Symbolically, they have been used to represent a challenge or an obstacle in an individual's life. There is much talk and literature about climbing this great symbolic trail but very little about the fact that reaching the top of any mountain is only a part of the process. One still must climb down without self-injury. What I refer to as "mercy mountains," are events in life that test your ability not only to scale up the side of the mountain but more importantly to successfully scale down, landing firmly and resolutely in your mental, spiritual, and physical capacities.

A mercy mountain can be grand or minute in scope based on your emotional and spiritual filters. As we enter into various phases in our life personally, professionally, and spiritually, we must confront our most private and intimate fears. God does give us the power to call the mountain to move but sometimes that is not the plan and we must take the practice journey, no matter how difficult, to conquer the greater mountain when it arises. Some of us do not move because we simply are not ready to grow – not yet anyway.

Mountains are coarse and often have very difficult terrains to navigate as is the process of life. Climbers often are bruised, cut, and battered along the way and very few ever reach the summit. Interestingly the word summit is used to describe a mountain peak and also to describe a high level conference or meeting to address pertinent social issues. Only seasoned and experienced experts sit on the stage or in the front of the conference area to demonstrate that they have mastered the summit in their chosen field.

Each individual will go through a number of life experiences that will propel them from one "mercy mountain" to another, for if you are not climbing up, you are scaling down, ping-ponging from the professional, to the personal, to the spiritual and back again. We do not necessarily choose some events but we must still deal with them as they arise and acknowledge that our reaction as well as our action is our choice.

The Discovery

At the age of 16, I met a young man that swept me off my feet and in the time span of about a year I found myself intimately involved. He was the most popular boy around, handsome and quite the charmer. I was the quiet, innocent and naïve Catholic school girl that had only had her first kiss a few months prior. It was well beyond my mental ability to understand anything more than he made me feel special and loved. I was pregnant at 17, scared, confused, and lonely. The security that should accompany a pregnancy and the creation of a new life was filled with anger, loss, more confusion, and uncertainty.

I spent many evenings curled in the fetal position – tears streaming down my face, hoping to wake up from this terrible dream and praying for God to take it all away. I feared my parents' reaction and their disappointment. I feared my friends' reactions and thoughts about who I was as a person. We inherently want to be known and perceived as a person of character but stereotypes are painfully difficult to break and are a part of everyday life. You can allow them to define you or you can define you and command respect. I knew that I would be thought of as ignorant, easy, and careless. And yes, I was careless but easy and ignorant, I was not. I had planned to terminate the pregnancy, never tell the young man and go about my life as if nothing had happened. We had since broken up and only spoke intermittently.

The same day I peed on a stick to see a pink plus sign brightly shine in the window, I walked into the senior hallway into a sea of sad faces.

I quickly grabbed one of my friends and said, "What happened, did somebody die?" half chuckling. She looked at me quite strangely and nodded.

My locker buddy for the past three years had been killed on impact in a car accident that weekend in the school parking lot. He was an only child and he had always made me laugh in the morning with his silly antics. I had been so engrossed in my own situation that I had tuned out the rest of the world. I walked to my locker solemnly. His locker was wrapped in black paper with a host of messages of love and sadness written on it in silver pen. The pen hung from the top of the locker, tied onto the groves, with a yellow ribbon. A group of seniors stood around the locker in a semi-circle – silent - and watched as one after another wrote their message.

One blonde haired girl shouted, "Where were you Saturday night?"

I turned around and pointed to myself, "Me?"

"Yeah, you. You're his locker buddy. We were all at ..." her voice began to shake and the tears began to fall.

"I was out. I didn't know. I'm sorry."

She regrouped and retorted. "Well, his real friends were there," and quickly turned away, flinging her hair into the face of the person passing her in the opposite direction. I began to cry, grabbed the pen, and wrote *I'll miss you. Your locker buddy.*

As a first generation Asian immigrant and the youngest of my family, I was the last great hope for an opportunity to reach the American dream of going to college. Neither of my sisters pursued an education past a high school diploma. My academic prowess made me a slam dunk to fulfill the hopes of my parents. I kept my secret to myself until the day of my locker buddy's funeral. I told my best male friend hoping for support. He looked at me in with a mixture of disgust, disappointment, and concern.

He only said, "When is the abortion scheduled, I'll go with you."

Our eyes locked for a brief moment. I turned and walked away. He shrugged his shoulders and resumed his conversation. We did not speak again until months later.

The following morning a special vigil was held for seniors only. As I left my home to drive to school one of my tires went flat. I was within a few blocks from where the father of my child worked and was desperate. There were a few inches of snow on the ground and snowflakes were still softly coming down. I walked into the store a bit dazed with my shoulders shrugged knowing that he would not receive me too kindly. The bell rang to announce my arrival and his head popped up from under the counter.

"What are you doing here?" he barked.

"I need your help."

"Call your parents! I'm at work."

"I can't. Can you please just help me this one time? I have to get to school. My friend died. Please?" My hands were clasped together and my eyes began to well up.

He looked at me, rolled his eyes, sighed and came from around the display. "Okay, what do you need?"

"My tire's flat. Can you just put on the donut so I can get to school?" I cracked a smile.

"Give me the keys." He reached out his hand.

I stood in the window and watched as he struggled to get the lug nuts off of the tire. He was pulling and pushing for some time until finally he threw down the tools and came back into the store.

"What the hell is this sh…," he waved his hands up and down and stormed into the back office area and screamed, "I'm not your rescuer anymore. Take care of it somewhere else."

The anger boiled inside of me and I blurted as he reentered the room, "Don't worry daddy, I intend to! Give me my keys."

"Wait, what did you just say?" He looked puzzled.

"You heard me. Just give me my keys. I wanna go home." I opened my hand and reached over the counter.

He hesitated, placed the keys in my hand and closed his hand around mine, looked at me and then my stomach. "Are you... really?"

"Does it matter? I'm taking care of it." I replied.

He paused. Let go of my hand and walked over to the newspaper. He grabbed the pen and began to doodle. He kept his head down.

"Are you sure, you want to? Well, you know... do that." There was silence.

"Yeah, I guess. What else am I going to do?"

"Keep it?"

I had not even thought of that option. "How... I can't. You..." as I began to cry uncontrollably.

He came from behind the counter, placed his hand under my chin, guided my face to his, stared me straight in the eyes and said, "Whatever you decide, I promise I will be there with you."

He then wrapped his arms around me and held me for a while. He went and changed the tire, and I left for school.

Later that evening, he called and asked, "Will you go to church with me this Sunday?"

My answer was, "Okay."

Sunday came and we were off to service at the Upper Room.

This was a church neither of us knew, more importantly we didn't know any of the parishioners. I was Catholic, and he was Pentecostal. This non-denominational setting was safe and a compromise between the two. Service was nearing its completion and the choir stood to sing the closing song. The minister called people who needed prayer to come to the altar. We both remained in our pew. As the choir sang, I felt an overflow of emotion. I began to walk toward the altar, but I didn't know why. I had been to a Pentecostal service where bodies fell one after another to the ground. I thought it was all dramatics.

I stood among the rows of people with tears, my body trembling. I saw the man approaching in his priestly vestment. I did not feel his touch but a flow of peace that I can only describe as a thick warm liquid that slowly engulfs you. At that very moment the child in my womb fluttered. I woke shaking on the floor with the tears still flowing, hoping that moment wouldn't end. A woman dressed all in white who appeared like she was floating helped me to my feet and when I looked over, the father of my child was also being helped to his feet. He reached out his hand and we walked back to our pew together.

As we drove home, we said very little. He held me and we sat in his mother's driveway for a while.

"So, what happens now?" he asked.

"I'm going to keep the baby. It moved today." I replied.

"Really?" He placed his hands on my belly. "Really?"

"Yeah, really. You don't have to stay with me."

"What are you saying?" he appeared confused.

"All I am saying is don't feel obligated to stay with me because I'm pregnant with your child. I'd rather be alone than have you here and leave halfway through the pregnancy. It'll hurt too much. I'll be okay."

I pulled away from his arms.

He held on tighter. "Let's try to make this work. I'm sorry for being such a jerk. I was scared."

"Scared of what?"

"Falling too fast," he whispered.

He pulled me closer and we cuddled for a while longer. He took me home, kissed me at the doorstep, and waved goodbye.

The following day, I called my sister in Pennsylvania. She was seven years my senior and I knew she'd help me through this. She kept pressuring me to tell my parents, but I refused. After I hung up the phone, I laid down on my bed and closed my eyes. The phone rang. I heard screaming in my native language and my name. Then, I heard heavy footsteps coming up the stairs, heading towards my room.

With the phone still in her hands, my mother said, "Tell me it's not true."

Just waking out of my sleep, I answered, "What?"

"Is your sister telling the truth, are you pregnant?" The tone of her voice grew to a loud screech.

"Give me the phone," I shouted. She threw the phone on my bed and stormed out the door.

I picked it up to hear my sister saying, "This is for the best. They need to know."

I hung up the phone, walked down the stairs and out the door. As I drove away, I saw my mother standing in the doorway.

This was my very first adult "mercy mountain." In a period of a few days, I was forced to make and cope with the decision of becoming a mother, disappointing myself and my family, hurting my parents who had taught me better, and hurting myself as I began the difficult journey of motherhood. I am often told by my spiritual elders that God will equip you and will never burden you beyond what you are capable to bare.

Four months later, I gave birth to a beautiful baby girl. She was born at the wee hours of the morning. Her delivery was prompted by a car accident the morning before and 13 hours of labor later she made her arrival into this world. She spent two weeks in the Neonatal Unit for jaundice treatments. She was feisty and kept pulling off her IV shades. We named her Destiny. Destiny's father and I stuck it out. The following year we were married, and we remain together to this day.

Due to the sheer height of a mountain, different segments of the mountain can rest in different climactic altitudes. As a result, the air thins out as you scale higher and higher minimizing the amount of oxygen present in the air. These layers or segments are referred to as life zones. Life zones function in a similar way for us as we grow in maturity. Spiritually we can persevere on a smaller amount of encouragement for our plate of assurance is fairly full and we are working off of an overflow but we must often return to the well to refill. The transition from one life zone to the next does not occur because you have reached another decade in your life, it does not occur because some magical creature keeps a record of your good deeds and you win a free pass once you hit a set number. We transpire once we are tested to move higher and we pass.

Aspiring Higher

Two years after my daughter's birth and the birth of my son in 1997, I sat in my hospital bed watching the funeral of Princess Diana. Her legacy for kindness and compassion outweighed her bad decisions and her problems. She persevered in helping others despite her conflict. It was at that moment that I decided to make an attempt to return to school so my children would be able to say mommy persevered despite her conflict. I had earned my high school diploma through home tutorial and was eligible to attend community college.

I arranged my work schedule so I could work the sum of a full work week between three jobs as a waitress, as a bank teller, and as a retail salesperson. I worked 12-hour days on Saturday and Sunday and an additional 10 hours between Monday and Thursday. I took 6 a.m. classes and returned home by 10 a.m. so my husband could leave for work. When he arrived home at 7 p.m., we'd have dinner and I would be out the door to go to a 9 p.m. evening class. I studied in between naps and during my time in the bathroom. I read homework assignments as bedtime stories and read during my breaks.

After my first semester, one professor who saw my ability nominated me for the Honor's program. I reluctantly went to meet with the Program Director. She was a plain woman who wore broom skirts and tie-dye shirts. Her hair was frizzed and she pushed all her female students to take a course on Feminism. I came to the meeting with my schedule ready. The schedule I planned around my life and my academic needs. As she began questioning my ability and assessing my lifestyle, she questioned why I chose to have classes so spaced out and why would I want to come to campus twice in one day when I could get it all done in one afternoon. One question led to another and then when I spoke of my children, she picked up my registration sheet and placed it on her desk. She made the following speech:

"I don't think you are Honor's Program material. You have far too many demands on your life at such a young age. Someone such as yourself could never achieve higher than a "C" average, statistically. I wish you all the best but I cannot in good conscience admit you into our accelerated courses and allow you to fail. As an educator it would be absolutely wrong, Thank you for your time."

She rose from her chair. After absorbing the shock, that this self-proclaimed feminist expressed such archaic thoughts, I rose from my chair, grabbed the registration form and ran in her pathway. She stopped and gasped at my audacity.

"Sign this!" I said firmly as I placed the form in her hand. "I have every right to be in this program. Maybe I had my kids young and maybe I have a lot of demands but so what. Statistics are not full proof. I can do the work."

She raised her eyebrows and said, "Impossible."

"If I receive a cumulative GPA of less than 3.5 you can kick me out of the program, and I will never enter your doorway again, but if I meet the mark, do not say another word to me and just advise me as any other student." I stared at her firmly and waited.

"Our requirement is only 3.0, and you will not be able to get higher than that," she retorted.

"Try me!"

"Okay, fine but don't say I didn't warn you." She grabbed the pen from my hand and signed the form.

I completed that semester with a 3.75 GPA and graduated 10 months later Magna Cum Laude.

At my induction to Phi Theta Kappa, the honor society for the two-year college, that same professor approached me and said, "You proved me wrong."

We have not spoken since. I was awarded a full scholarship to Stonybrook University, and as the 1999-2000 school year began, I received a request to apply to Columbia University.

Initially, I just kept rubbing my hand over the embossed Columbia insignia thinking, imagine if this actually happened. About a week later, my husband and I went to an information session to learn more about the cost and if there were potential scholarships. We were greeted by hip and trendy Manhattanites who explained in great detail the benefits of a Columbia University education but there was very limited scholarship opportunity with the largest scholarship amounting to ten thousand dollars, which was barely enough to pay for three classes.

I decided to apply to have the satisfaction of knowing that I could get into a school of Columbia's stature, but had no intention of going there. Two weeks later I received a letter of acceptance and a phone call.

The voice on the other line was a jubilant young woman who stated, "You are a candidate for a substantial scholarship."

My response was, "How do you define substantial?"

She giggled, "I'm not sure yet, but we will know soon."

We hung up the phone and continued on as if I were beginning at Stonybrook University by mailing in my student fee to secure my slot. A week before Labor Day, I received a message to call Columbia's admissions team. During my lunch break at work, I drove to my mother's job where my Godfather was the acting pastor. We went downstairs and I made the call.

We went through the usual cordial greeting and then she asked, "Are you sitting down?"

"No, but just give me the news straight," I said anxiously.

"You have been chosen as the first recipient of the Program for Academic Leadership and Service, which is a full scholarship to the university, the first of its kind. Congratulations!"

I was silent for a brief moment and then began jumping up and down. My mother and Godfather stood next to me ready to burst.

"Are you there?"

"Yes," cracking a huge smile. "Thank you sooo much."

"No, thank you for being such a great candidate. We will see you at orientation," she answered.

I slowly placed the phone onto its base and began shouting and screaming in the rectory basement.

"I'm going to Columbia!!!!" I shouted over and over again.

"What happened?" asked my Godfather as he put his hands on my shoulders to keep me still.

"I've been awarded a full scholarship. The first of its kind."

My Godfather leaped for joy as my mother wept. I quickly grabbed the phone and called my husband whose screams could be heard across the phone wire.

Excitement can barely describe the joy that filled my heart. I struggled to maintain that humility throughout my academic career at Columbia University. There were many instances were I was placed in the limelight. My strength and perseverance were driven by my gratefulness for the gift of the scholarship, the gift of the education, and the gift of God's favor. My first six months as a Columbian was chaotic, frightening and ecstatic all mixed into one strange feeling. In the beginning many administrators were unsure if I could actually be successful. I was often reminded of the honor to receive the scholarship and the conditions that would cause me to lose it. Not only did I have to maintain above a 3.0 GPA but I also had to volunteer and make an impact as a public servant. Over time I began public speaking sharing my story with future Columbians and the local community members.

I often returned home from school exhausted at 10 p.m. My days rolled one into the other. Ollie's chicken and string beans lunch special with brown sauce functioned as both lunch and dinner. The fortune cookie or cookies on occasion were my desserts. I always kept enough change in my pocket to buy one coffee each day. The hard square shaped padded chairs in the student common were my nap area. Reading was as inherent as breathing as it inundated every free moment of my time. I guess that was me receiving my just desserts majoring in English Literature and Writing and having to write two thesis papers. When someone asks me how I did it, how I was able to survive the rigors and the fast pace of an Ivy League education, my answer was simply this *"only by God's grace."*

The endless hours of writing, editing, and reading, deciphering and interpreting could never out weigh my desire to finish what I had started – to earn my college degree. Two years seemed to have occurred in a measure of a week. Those that doubted my abilities in the beginning of my tenure were the same persons that affectionately hugged and cheered for me on commencement week. The whirlwind of watching your life's desire come to pass is euphoric; it lifts you above the clouds.

Graduation brought with it the culminating moment where all the sleepless nights, all the sweat induced exam anxiety, and all the gut wrenching presentations were the battle scars of a job well done. My Godfather and my husband were Abbott and Costello on class day, knocking each other over in excitement to get in the best position for that "moment of truth" photo. The photo when you walked crossed the stage garbed in your blue and white gown, head held high, smiling from ear to ear as your tassel swings to and fro, making the transformation from student to alumna. Commencement brought with it a Citation, Degree Honors, and a Recognition Certificate for Student Service.

The Columbia Record wrote a feature story on my journey to and through Columbia and I began to tout myself. I began to refer to the successes in my life as mine alone. I momentarily forgot the many blessings and grace-filled moments that led to this achievement. My summit experience was brief, a matter of a few weeks, before I tumbled down the mountain and struck the ground of reality hard. I think I even had a concussion. I had been so enraptured with the process of completing my degree that I had not adequately prepared myself for entry into the workforce, taking the first position that came my way. Shortly after graduation, the organization decided to dissolve the position and I found myself unemployed for the first time in my life. I've worked since I was 12 years old. My first job was as a receptionist and a sacristan for my church. Many jobs came my way but blinded by my own blown up ego, those positions were beneath me. In the book, "The Arrogance of Power," the author talks of how power can corrupt the mind and can cause a false sense of invincibility. I fell victim to this and hit the ground hard. A few months later, my husband had been granted a great opportunity. He traveled to India to conduct call center trainings for a private agency. His flight departed on September 8, 2001. On the morning of September 11, 2001, I received a frantic call from my Godfather.

He shouted, "Turn on Channel 4. Turn on Channel 4."

I quickly put on the television and sat on my mother's bed. My mother soon joined me. I held the phone to my ear but there was only a muted silence as we watched the Twin Towers get struck by commercial airplanes and crumble. The tears fell faster than words and my Godfather began to pray. I simply listened, said Amen at the close and hung up the phone. After sitting quietly for several minutes, I jumped up from the bed and began dialing my husband's cell number. I couldn't get through. The remainder of the day remains a blur until the moment the phone rang late in the evening and my husband's voice was on the other line.

"Are you all okay? Are you okay?" he repeated nervously.

"We're fine. Are you okay? "

"I'm in a safe house at the U.S. Embassy. I don't know when I'll be coming home. I'll call back soon. Love you." His voice grew softer. "Bye."

He flew home three weeks later. The remainder of his staff did not return home until two weeks later. The whole world seemed to shift that day. People, for a while anyway, began to take extra time to say hello, to hug the ones they loved, and to recommit to the Lord. I humbled myself and took a part time position with a medical billing firm. My responsibilities grew as the owner saw my abilities and I began to learn the business and create presentation packages for the main sales team. I continued to apply for full-time work and I waited patiently knowing that those directly impacted by September 11th would probably get first preference but that was okay. I waited and waited.

Vonekham Phanithavong-Guthrie

An Act of Love

In 1979, a young priest touched by the devastation of the Vietnam War and its impact to the people of Southeast Asia decided to take on a grand mission. He was referred to as the "altar boy" priest because of his youthful appearance. His stature was small but he stood tall in his faith and committed in his mission. Meeting after meeting, he appealed to his associates and the laity of his church to partner with him to make the project God had given him come to pass. Ten families agreed to commit themselves and their time to helping a family affected by the Vietnam War, and the church made the decision to adopt a family and bring them to America. His name was Fr. Larry. Hundreds of applications for sponsorship came across his desk and he and his staff reviewed each with precision but he could only save one. He chose my family – a young mother with three young daughters who were in a refugee camp in Thailand. Paperwork was completed, a residence erected in the church's convent basement, employment secured through Catholic Charities, and tuition waived for private academic instruction for the children.

On a brisk morning in the fall at around 1 a.m. – my family stepped onto American soil for the first time. My mother unable to speak a word of English simply nodded and smiled at the new faces before her. She held my sister's hand and my eldest sister carried me in her arms. Our clothes were mismatched and did not fit us correctly. Our stomachs were swollen from malnutrition and our faces pale. My mother tells the story of how we were guided to a car and drove many miles to a large brick building with two sticks on its wall one horizontal and the other laid on top in a vertical position. A gray haired woman was sweeping the front steps as we approached this large building. The woman opened the door that had colorful glass on it and directed us to a large table with many chairs where all forms of food were prepared. As the youngest, three years of age, I climbed down from my sister's arms and ran to the table. My mother reprimanded me. All I knew was that I was hungry and had

40

never seen so much food in my life. I was only six months old when we fled our country, Laos, and I had known nothing but hunger.

Fr. Larry smiled and held my mother's hand to ease her worry. He brought her over to the table and gestured for her to eat. She called my sisters and I over to the table and handed each of us half a hard-boiled egg. In the refugee camp, my mother, gave us each a quarter of one hard-boiled egg each day and about two spoonfuls of rice. Fr. Larry repeated the gesture for us to eat. It only took two times for my sisters and me to get the message, and we ate and we ate. I was told as a young adult that on that first day in America I ate ten hard-boiled eggs. I threw them up later. There were many other choices on the table but the only food I had knowledge of was the hard-boiled egg. I later learned of the many foods that America has to offer to a hungry young child and my stomach now swells for other reasons.

Years passed, and Fr. Larry assumed the role of our Godfather, treating us like his own offspring, ensuring we received opportunity, culture and love. He celebrated birthdays with us, taught us how to read, disciplined us, and spoiled us. My sisters and I were raised in the basement of a convent. Our bedroom lay below the chapel. Our playground was the hallways of the rectory and the storage area we called the cubby hole. Fr. Larry even loved us so much that he let us go. When my mother discovered that my father was alive and living in France. He did all he could to reunite us and he stepped back and allowed us to become a family again. The transition was extremely difficult for me as the youngest child. Fr. Larry was the only father I knew. I became angry with him for not being around. I thought he stopped loving me and at the time, he was doing what he thought was best.

He still remained a part of our lives but he respected our father as the head of the family and did not over step his boundaries. When the family vacations ended, all we had left was our annual summer trip to Great Adventure and some outings here and there. I recall the first time Fr. Larry took me to a Jets football game. He packed up some homemade crumb cake and hot chocolate. He had in the trunk of his car a full assortment of scarves, hats and gloves in a plastic milk carton. It had to have been 30 or 40 degrees out and as we drove to the stadium, he took a scenic route. He made a couple of stops along the way, handing out the winter items to the homeless on the streets of New York. I do not recall the score of the game, and I only vaguely remember how cold I was sitting in the bleeder seats he loved so much but I will never forget his kindness that day or the importance of helping those less fortunate.

A few days before his death, Fr. Larry had returned home from vacation in Thailand. He called me excited.

I remember the booming sound of his voice as he said his usual greeting, "This is your Goooood Faaather."

He told me of how he received specialized training for a new suicide intervention program with the Air Force and that he wanted me to tag team with him to do the presentations. I, of course, agreed. He went on and on about how my story could save lives and how God was going to use me. We had decided to meet for breakfast on Tuesday to go over the details. He was gunned down and murdered at Monday during mass.

We received word from Larry's family that the wake services were to be held around the clock at the church where he had been shot. My sisters arrived the following afternoon and we attended the evening service. Our neighbors kept my children that night. Fr. Larry's wake was closed to the media though they swarmed the premises hoping to catch a glimpse of his body. I had yet to cry. My husband stayed close by my side. He knew what was soon to come. I consoled my mother and my sisters at our home and in the car. As we walked into the church foyer, I stopped. My husband gently grabbed my arm. I did not budge. My mother and sisters went before me and began descending down the center aisle. I hung back in the rear of the church looking at cards and letters of love written by the children in his parish's school. My husband followed me. I finally mustered up the courage to walk down the aisle with my husband following a pace behind me.

As my eyes connected with the lifeless body that lay in the raised coffin, my body filled up with such fevered emotion.

My legs could not hold me up and I fell into the arms of the parishioner in the pew, a family friend, shouting, "No! No! Nooooo!"

She held me as I collapsed onto the pew's seat and my husband wrapped his arms around my waist and hugged me from behind. Fr. Larry's family came to console me.

His sister-in-law hugged me and said, "You were his baby girl. When you graduated from Columbia Larry called us on his cell. He was on his way to the train, so excited, he said, "My baby girl did it. She did it."

I cried for most of that service. After all the crowds left each evening the family was provided with a private viewing. Larry's family knew how much he loved us and allowed us to be apart of that time. When we returned home that evening my husband shut the blinds. We put the phone on mute and everyone went to bed without saying a word. The following morning, my mother frantically woke us up at 6 a.m. for the morning vigil service. My sisters rolled over and went back to bed. My mother persisted.

At the time, I was angry and all the anger inside of me burst out onto my mother and I yelled, "This is not only about you."

She was devastated and my sisters woke to come to her aid. They never scolded me but just ignored my rants. After service, we went to the rectory for coffee and breakfast. The anger still brewing in me, I saw many unfamiliar faces sitting in the rectory. Nieces and nephews, their girlfriends, etc. One young male cousin spoke of how he would miss him.

I looked at him, knowing I had never seen him and asked, "What is your last memory of Larry?"

His response was, "I haven't seen him in seven years." My husband grabbed my arm and squeezed tightly.

I smiled and walked away.

Later that afternoon, we received a call from the Associated Press and I answered the call with "no comment." So much had been alleged in the murder and the media was hoping to find a villain in Fr. Larry as this was around the time when the Catholic church was receiving a great deal of negative press over acts of pedophilia.

The following morning, exhausted I answered a phone call. On the other end of the line was a familiar voice, a voice from my childhood. It was the priest that resided in the convent when I was a child. He asked for me.

I answered, "This is."

He responded coldly, "Why aren't you speaking out? You are an ungrateful godchild. You should be giving thanksgiving for all Fr. Larry did for you."

I did not know how to respond and hung up the phone.

Immediately, I called Fr. Bob, my mother's boss, my pastor at the time. I told him of the phone call and my confusion as to what to do.

His answer was this, "Do what your heart tells you. Larry knew you loved him." I thanked him and left it at that.

A knock came on the front door. It was *Newsday*. When asked how they were given our address the name of the same priest that had scolded me was provided. I was the chosen spokesperson for my family. The interview was short and as the reporter fished for dirt. I looked at him and said, "You will find nothing. He was a saint."

The questions ended and the story ran as the feature story the following day. When we entered the church the morning of Fr. Larry's funeral, one of his dear friends had arrived from Oregon and she sang to him one last time. I mustered up the courage to walk up to the coffin, pressed my fingers to my lips, kissed them and touched his hand. I whispered, "Goodnight daddy," and walked away.

That was the first time I called him daddy out loud since my father arrived in America. His funeral was as grand as his love for life and for people. I cried in my husband's arms uncontrollably when they lowered the coffin and closed it. I never cried again when I was awake after that moment. The cathedral was standing room only and the burial procession was marked with respect, love and reverence. After the bagpipes finished playing and taps was blown, gunshots were fired, and two Air Force fighter jets flew overhead, Larry was laid to rest.

Each town that was passed through had two fire trucks, ladders extended, and a United States flag hung from its helm. Rows of Air

Force officers stood in full garb, in a salute position as the hearse drove passed. It was magnificent. I had found out a week earlier that I was pregnant with my third child but had yet to announce it to the family. My husband worried for my emotional and physical heath. He immediately escorted me back to our car after the prayer concluded. We spent that evening sharing stories of all the silly things he had done over the years. Fr. Larry was quite the practical joker.

About two weeks later, I was called in for an interview and a month later I was employed full-time in the healthcare field. One night in a dream, Larry spoke to me. It felt so real like the conversation actually occurred. The dream helped me to know he was okay and in heaven. He was dressed in his khaki cargo pants with extra pockets and a snug t-shirt, hiking boots and a camera around his neck. He told me to come and sit with him on the steps leading up to my bedroom. We sat and joked and laughed. He said, why are you worried? I'm fine. I am on the vacation of a lifetime. The eternal trip I've been waiting for my entire life. Then he said, by the way there are two. He smiled, kissed and hugged me and vanished. Initially, I thought I was pregnant with twins but the following month my sister announced she too was pregnant. Five months later, my Lauren arrived.

Fr. Larry's funeral was the last time I step foot into church until another family funeral. My anger and fear would not allow it. I blamed God for all the wrong in my life. Ten months later my mother-in-law passed suddenly. My husband was distraught as we made the decision to turn off the life support. My mother-in-law's pastor, Bishop Brown and his wife visited her in the ICU and gave her last rites. The day of her demise, Bishop Brown came to my home and prayed with our family. He made all the arrangements and directed us on what to do and how to do it. I observed all that was occurring and overwhelmed by the love my husband received from this man. I had numerous interactions with the Bishop. He officiated at my wedding but this was different and it stayed with me.

The anniversary of Fr. Larry's death came and passed. I was awoken by nightmares and a moist pillowcase. My husband later told me of how he would watch me as I cried in my sleep and hold me. More months passed and another year was upon us. My husband went to watch night service with his father that New Year's Eve despite my pleading with him to stay home with me. I laid in my bed after having tucked the children in for the night. My phone rang and it was my husband checking in. I attempted to go back to sleep. At about 5 minutes to midnight, I felt a tremendous weight on my chest. I felt as if I was suffocating. I couldn't catch my breath. Fear over ran me and I panicked. I thought to myself – *I am going to die. Right here, right now, alone.* The presence I felt was evil. I tried to scream but no sound came from my voice. I struggled and then Fr. Larry flashed into my mind. *Call on Jesus. I screamed over and over JESUS in my head.* The weight lifted and was gone in seconds. I called me husband.

He answered, "Happy New Years, baby."

My voice winded, I said, "Something happened tonight. Something bad,"

"I'm on my way home."

When he arrived home, I told him of the experience. He held me, kissed my forehead and we went to sleep.

Another anniversary of Larry's death arrived, and I was still unable to be happy. Now, I cried at the drop of a hat if a memory was triggered. I couldn't even drive through the town he was murdered in. I sought the counsel of my pastor. We had a few sessions. He worried for me because it was far beyond the natural mourning stages. I told him how I felt God had abandoned me. I told him how angry I was and how I felt cheated. I spoke of how I missed Larry. We scheduled one last meeting where Father Tim was going to give me a list of professional counselors. We sat in the new dining area of the rectory and as he spoke I looked up at a picture of The Last Supper. The image of Jesus pierced my heart and I heard in a whisper, *"Remember me."* I jumped, startled.

Fr. Tim put his hand out to touch mine and asked, "Are you alright?"

"I have it. I have it," I exclaimed.

"Have what?" he inquired.

"Why I have been so sad, why I feel so alone?" I smiled. "The killer not only killed Larry he killed me, my faith, I mean. It's my faith, my faith I'm missing."

Fr. Tim smiled and hugged me. My next challenge was returning to church.

After tumbling down the side of the mountain for such a long time, I was bruised all over emotionally and spiritually. God's mercy allows us one chance after the other to get it right. His grace protects us from fatal injury as described in my New Year's experience. When you turn your face from the Lord, you enter a world of chaos, emptiness and despair. Know that with every mountain there is a new horizon and new beginnings, though frightening, birth each of us in to more beautiful, more vibrant human beings. As we dust off our bodies and begin to stand up again, remember we sometimes must crawl before we can walk. Strength grows over time, one step at a time.

Music has always been a powerful element in my life and for three or four minutes in my day it allows me to escape to a place where all is good with the world, where people dance in joy, where we encourage and inspire each other, where there is no judgment from others. It has helped me to heal during the most difficult moments in my life and helped me to keep pressing on when life had smothered me so that I wanted to throw in the towel. Yolanda Adams song "Fragile Heart" and Ce Ce Winans song "Mercy Said No" helped me to heal and be able to cope with my loss and the understanding of why God allowed this tragedy to happen.

Chapter Four: What's Great About Me?

One of the concepts many people grapple with including me is self-worth and self-esteem. This chapter provides an exercise and demonstrates ways in which you can deal with thoughts of doubt, insecurity and a poor self-image. Every culture teaches their youth differently. I did not grow up with a church youth mother like my children have who steps in and reinforces good values, who exemplifies true goodness and who my children love so dearly that they do not want to disappoint her.

In many ways, she has also become a mother to me. As a child I had two wonderful women in my life, my natural mother and my Godmother. In Christianity, every child that is baptized has appointed Godparents, some more than one set. Almost like extra insurance. Not all people that take on this role live up to it. A Godparent is supposed to help the parents raise the child with Godly values. I had a Godmother that was strict yet wonderfully loving. I called her Clairey. She was one of the wisest women I knew.

My mother had been through a great deal in her lifetime. She is the most courageous person I know, loving in spite of the circumstance and giving. She carried the lessons she received as a child and passed them onto my sisters and me. In our home country, Laos, women in short, are second-class citizens. Citizens subservient to their male counterparts, raised to become wives and mothers, to serve their in-laws and their husband. They were never to touch a man's head – this was a sign of deep disrespect that could bring on a beating that would be acceptable. A woman always had to keep her head below her spouses demonstrating his dominance. The man always ate first and was served upon. This was... is a part of my culture whether right or wrong – it doesn't matter. My mother instilled those same lessons in me. My Godmother and my education instilled American lessons of independence. Both remained in conflict for me for many, many years.

Am I worthy? This question haunts many on a daily basis. Success is an experience that warrants and validates a sense of worth but before success can occur you must be fervent that the affirmation of your worth is a mandate for others. It may sound arrogant but others will not begin to see your value unless you place before them the expectation of how you should be valued. This can be done both verbally and non-verbally.

On Time

Shauna fresh from her graduation week was in route to a second interview with the Director of Admissions for a state university. Ecstatic she arrived to the interview 15 minutes early, a whole extra five minutes than recommended by the adviser at her college's career center. The meeting was scheduled for 10 a.m. and in the back of her mind, Shauna kept remembering that she only had a two hour window because she had to pick up her infant daughter so her mother could get to work on time. The minutes went by slowly and Shauna sat in the waiting area, her back pressed up against the chair, her legs crossed to one side and her palms were beginning to sweat. She rubbed her hands against the side of her skirt pretending to straighten herself up to dry her palms.

Before long 10 a.m. came and went. The time was inching toward 10:15 a.m. Shauna approached the desk and inquired about the delay.

"Good morning again," she said smiling. "I have a 10 a.m. interview with Dean Reese Matthews and as it's 10:15 I was curious if you could give me a time line as to when you might be expecting her?" She smiled again.

"Oh, I'll check," replied the receptionist.

Shauna stood and waited and waited and waited. The receptionist got up from her desk and went to speak with an officer, closing the door behind her. She soon returned to her desk.

"Miss. I have some information for you."

"Yes."

"Dean Matthews was called to an emergency meeting and should be here shortly."

"Thank you." Shauna smiled and went back to her seat.

Another 30 minutes passed and still no sign of the Dean and the time was 10:45 a.m. Shauna was getting worried. She needed a job and this was the one she really, really wanted. It was close to home and paid a half way decent wage.

She once again approached the receptionist's desk. "I'm sorry to bother you but would you have an update on when the Dean might be arriving for this interview?"

"I'm sorry. I really don't know but I am sure she is on her way. Please take a seat and as soon as she arrives I will be sure to let her know your hear."

"Thank you."

Agitated, Shauna went back to her seat. This receptionist had not even informed the Dean of her arrival. She began to fidget in her chair – a pre-interview no no – but she had difficultly hiding her agitation. Another 30 minutes passed, and like a storm, an older Caucasian woman came through the office doors with dusty brown hair wearing a Jones New York tweed suit. She darted to an office in the back of the room. Shauna thought to herself in summer, tweed? Really? Ten more minutes passed before Shauna was called to go to Dean Matthews's office.

Dean Matthews extended her hand and said, "Hi, you must be Shauna. So sorry for the delay. Please sit down." She gestured to a small couch in her office.

They both took a seat after they shook hands. Shauna smiled, sat down, placed one foot in front of the other, leaned over into her briefcase, pulled out a folder, opened it and folded her hands on top of the folder.

"If you would allow me..." she said. Dean Matthews nodded.

"Due to the delay in the start of this interview, I only have about 20 minutes to speak with you as I have another appointment at 12 p.m. Is it possible for us to reschedule?"

"Absolutely not, then you better wow me in 20 minutes to get this job. I will not be conducting interviews after this week. I'd suggest you change your other appointment - I'll give you a few minutes to do so – and do this interview," the Dean retorted.

A bit angered Shauna took a deep breath to prevent from smacking the woman and smiled. "I can not reschedule my appointment. Twenty minutes it is then." Shauna replied.

The Dean noticeably agitated, put her hands on her lap. "Okay, so right off the bat you are not demonstrating something I expect from all my staff – the team player mentality. Convince me otherwise," the Dean barked.

Angry now, Shauna closed her folder, leaned down and placed it in her briefcase, stood up, extended her hand and said, "Thank you for your time. I am not interested in this position. It is evident that my interpretation of the team player mentality differs from yours. You are the leader and your blatant disrespect for my time is not what a team leader should exemplify. It's obvious this is not a fit." Shauna extended her hand.

The Dean waved it aside. "You are pretty brazen for an unemployed recent grad." She walked over to her desk and said, "Please see yourself to the door."

Shauna walked out and shut the door behind her.

About a year later, Shauna learned that Dean Matthews was fired and at the time of her interview, had only been in the position about four months.

No matter your age, gender, ethnicity or religious beliefs, you have a right to be respected but you must demand and set your boundaries. Shauna understood that her time was just as valuable as the Dean's and though not taking the meeting meant she'd be unemployed for a little while longer, actually a long while longer. Her self-respect and self-worth was more important. It set a precedent on how she would be treated in the future by this potential new boss.

On Time – Part II

Three years pasted and Shauna found herself unemployed again, but now she had two children to support and a husband. It had been over a year and Shauna had gone on more than a dozen of interviews but was always told the same thing either she was overqualified or the offered salary was ridiculously low. She was called for yet another interview with a large organization that was also close to home. She arrived to the interview and was greeted by the Program Director.

The Director was a well-dressed J. Crew fan, fairly approachable and even smiled when she extended her hand for a handshake. "Hi, my name is Allison. Just let me say, you have a great resume. We are in the process of expanding our department and need someone like yourself with strong know-how and experience."

The conversation continued for about 20 minutes. Shauna thought that Allison had good intentions and believed her discussion of her team approach to the department's workflow. The salary posted was low but the benefits were good and Shauna got four weeks vacation and a number of other perks. Plus, her family desperately needed the money, as the cupboards were getting scarce. So, when offered the job, at a reasonable salary, Shauna accepted.

The first three months with the organization were non-eventful and Shauna had developed some friendships. The team approach that was spoken of in the interview only existed in words and not in actions. Shauna often worked independently and with little directives. She soon realized and learned that her Director in fact had less experience than her, even though she was about 30 years her senior. Shauna's three month review was presented to her and in the review Allison had noted that all of Shauna's work was adequate except one area — her ability to write. Shauna's career and gift was her unique writing style. After she calmed down, Shauna refuted the review in writing and had a talk with Allison who explained that she felt that Shauna had more room to grow as a writer.

Three more months passed and the relationship between Shauna and Allison became more strained. The breaking point came when Shauna had worked on a large project for four weeks and then had a feeling something was wrong and in fact she was right. Allison had given Shauna the wrong project identification number and Shauna had been preparing an entirely different presentation that required specific technical needs. This all occurred the day before the project was due to leadership. Shauna stayed at the office late that evening to make the needed changes and had the project ready for submission the following morning.

Shauna's six month review was due, and Allison wrote how Shauna had not time managed her work well and highlighted the special project Shauna had worked on to hand in on time. Shauna could no longer hold her tongue and prepared the emails and other evidence that proved Allison's error in instruction. Senior leadership was involved to mediate the discussion but the politics that surrounded Allison's appointment tied the senior leadership's hands for the department.

Shauna resigned shortly thereafter. The experience taught her to never take a position out of an emotional need for the months that were loss in that organization could have been used somewhere where she would be appreciated and a part of a true team.

On Time – Part III

Some years later, Shauna found herself back on the job search track. She now had real experience behind her, two directorships and respect in her industry. She had taken a year off from full-time work to raise her son and only took intermittent consulting work as it came before her. At the time, the only positions around were at the mid-management level and Shauna thought this might work thinking maybe I'll actually get to leave the office at a decent hour. As a director she had sweated through 12 hour days, pressed through 24-hour projects and knew what it meant to be on call, even over the weekends. She was not looking for that type of grueling schedule. She came across an advertisement for a management position at a local firm in her region. Though not an advocate of sending out resumes blindly she did for this particular position.

After passing the phone interview stage, she felt very confident the Recruiter liked her, they scheduled a face-to face interview with management for the following week. Again, Shauna arrived early expecting to have to fill out an application for employment. First, she sat down with the Recruiter and they spoke about the job expectations in broad strokes. Soon the recruiter's phone rang and Shauna was escorted to the Vice President's office. Shauna thought it odd that she would be interviewing with the Vice President first.

As she entered the office, a neatly dressed woman rose from her desk, walked around, extended her hand and said, "Welcome, my name is Madeline Divers. Please come and sit down so we can talk a little bit."

Shauna shook her hand as she said, "Shauna Crews, so very nice to meet you."

The Vice President took her over to a round table and gestured for her to take a seat. Shauna observed Madeline. She was very regal, her jewelry did not shout out I need more pay and she had such a sweet disposition. Shauna thought *wait she's going to low ball the salary... this is all a set up.* The two women spoke for some time. They laughed and before long an hour had passed. Madeline thanked Shauna not once but twice for taking the time to come in for the interview. When the discussion of salary came up, Shauna's range was accepted.

They both got up from the table, shook hands and Madeline said, "We will most definitely be in touch real soon."

The Recruiter was standing by the doorway. She asked Shauna to wait outside the door for just a few minutes and then brought her to another office to meet with the Director of Human Resources. Shauna watched as a young assertive woman came through the doorway. Shauna could feel her confidence just by how she entered the room.

The Director extended her hand, "Hi Shauna, my name is Detrick Collins, so very nice to meet you. I just have a few quick questions and you'll be all set."

Shauna stood up and said, "I'm Shauna Crews, so very nice to meet you too."

The two spoke for about 20 minutes. Detrick's approach was straight and to the point. You could tell she was trained in the corporate world. They had good conversation and Shauna was even able to get Detrick to smile for a moment during their talk. Six weeks passed and Shauna had not received a call. One afternoon while spending time with a friend getting a pedicure at the local nail salon Shauna's cell phone rang. It was the call she had been waiting for.

The voice on the other end of the line said, "We would like to have you join our team."

Shauna could barely contain herself and asked, "What offer are we looking at?"

The organization was generous for the position they were seeking to fill and Shauna gladly joined the team.

These three stories mirror each other in some ways. In each "On Time," there are three different types of leaders. I refer to them with the following titles: arrogant leader; insecure leader and true leader. The arrogant leader did not recognize or did not care to recognize that she was the spearhead of a team effort. She ostracized a potential team member and did not respect her time. As a leader, you are the walking, breathing example. If you are careless with time or don't give respect to your colleagues, you are endangering your progress, the company's progress and the department's progress. Leaders, in many ways live in a glass house, being watched and mimicked by their subordinates. If you respect others and demonstrate loyalty to concepts of integrity and hard work, your team will stand with you, even if you falter, out of loyalty and gratitude. At the end of the day **leadership is character that does not waver**.

The insecure leader in "One Time – Part II," the manager misrepresented herself, her ability to lead and her work style. This leader often gains their position either by default rather than through true merit or has been placed in the position for a political reason, often due to nepotism. Also, Shauna was operating in fear due to her current situation. She lowered her standards and suffered for doing that with seven months of working under a person who was unqualified and not capable to help her develop as a professional or an a person. One factor that you should always weigh in on is your decision to apply for a company is, who will be leading you and are you working to learn or working to earn? Can he or she teach you anything? If it's through direct mentoring – wonderful – or through observation, your supervisor should be someone with the expertise and experience that will help you grow as an individual and a professional.

The executives in "On Time - Part III" are the true leaders. They understood these concepts well and that is why this type of organization thrives even in this very difficult economic climate. If you notice not only did Shauna's direct supervisor emulate these traits so did the human resources team showing that the culture of the organization supported growth via professional development and they understood the importance of hiring good, solid talent. Shauna was made to feel that her contribution and ability to grow as part of this organization's team would be a positive experience.

When seeking employment, we enter into a process with our potential new financial source and a group of people we will be spending more time with than our own families when you calculate the hours spent on a full-time work schedule. You should work within an environment that celebrates your talents but is also able to provide you with unbiased criticism that will allow you to enhance your weaker skills. Part of the hiring process involves having to fill out a detailed application, a staple and legal mandate of all employers. The application provides the employer some basic information that they can then use to validate and confirm, through various sources, your truthfulness.

In short, are you who you say you are? And can you do what you say you can do? In a word – credentials. Employment candidates often take the time to fill out the application with care to ensure they put their best foot forward. The next step is the interview, where you now have to verbally demonstrate you are the one for the job. The employer is seeking a fit in skill and talent but also in personality, presentation and work ethic. When we go through difficult stages in life such as a layoff, divorce, loss of a loved one, illness, etc. some begin to question their abilities to do the job; be able to be loved; find joy; and be strong. No matter whether you are employed or not, you remain who you are. Below is an exercise that I hope will help you to remember you are a talented, worthy and wonderful human being even when the world is not so kind around you. When you begin to question your worth or ability, take out this completed exercise to remind you just how great you are.

Personal Assurance Application:

Last Name: _____

First Name: _____

Address: _____

_____

City: _____ State: _____

Zip Code: _____

Personal Skills:

1. Are you a good, trustworthy and dependable person?

   Yes/ No

2. Do you avoid confrontation or face it as a challenge to be addressed quickly and without incident?

   Yes/ No

3. Are you still hurting from something that happened over a year ago?

   Yes/ No

4. Do you forgive wholeheartedly?

   Yes/ No

5. Are you able to be in a room with someone that has hurt you and not feel angry inside?

   Yes/ No

6. Do you live each day to be a blessing?

   Yes/ No

7. Do you search for truth and if you find it, do you accept it?

   Yes/ No

8. Do you smile everyday – (a genuine smile)?

   Yes/ No

9. Which comes first – your needs, the needs of others or the needs of God? _____

10. Do you focus on what's yet to come, what is or what was? ____

    _____

11. Are your gifts in use or are they stagnant? _____

    _____

12. Do you stand firm in the midst of others trying to tear you down? _____

Chapter 5: Life's Glue

When working under a team approach in business, the first thing you learn is that productivity does not happen in silos. Each team member is responsible and accountable for the other and the quality of his or her performance. When one is weak in his or her assignment, the others should cover him or her and help them to grow in their lack of skill. As the old adage says, "You are only as strong as your weakest link." This same practice should be applied to everyday life. Who is part of your team? In sports, every team member has a specific role in order for the team to win. In football, only the quarterback can throw the ball and as he surveys the lay of the playing field, he tosses the ball to that individual he thinks has the most promising situation to make the catch and who also has demonstrated the talent in the past and can maneuver through a difficult set of blockers. Life is very much the same way. In your life, sometimes you need to pass the ball and allow others to shine and run for the winning goal. There are moments when you will get center stage and moments when you need to be content to step back, support and celebrate others.

As the old Birds song says, "With every day, turn, turn, turn there is a season turn, turn..." Life is much the same way. With life comes the realization that death is a given. I've lost some very close and important individuals in my life, for some it was simply time, for others tragedy stepped in and it was very unexpected.

This book is dedicated to three very special individuals who all passed on within a period of five years from 2000 to 2005. Fr. Larry was my bedrock, my daddy. He raised me and molded me into the woman I am today – focused, sometimes hard headed but always caring and thoughtful. Clairey, as I called her, was the person who always had wisdom to share. If I ever had a quandary, she'd always have the answer and if she didn't have the answer, she'd tell me to pray my rosary. Maureen was a free spirit. We were best friends since the age of three, often referred to as ying and yang with her blond hair and blue/ gray eyes and me with my jet black hair and dark brown eyes. She loved the Grateful Dead and I loved Boys II Men. In many ways we would be considered polar opposites, but we were always there for each other, even when the other didn't want us to be. The loss of these special individuals was difficult, and I still miss each of them daily but life has a way of healing such wounds in very unique ways, which is described in the following stories.

A Father's Love

Since the age of three, the only man that I knew as the closest thing to a dad was my Godfather – Fr. Larry. As I grew in age, I dropped the Father part of his title and just called him Larry. He was a practical joker; an individual that loved life and adventure; he was the original Diego – exploring the world and he toured the entire globe not once but twice; he was supportive, loving and, at all times, walked in the words and principles of the Bible.

He gave to me a love for people, God, reading and the written word. As a child, I used to watch television in his room, only after my homework was done, while I waited for my mother to finish her day at work. I recall one afternoon when he showed me a book about famous women. He pointed out one in particular, she was not beautiful in the conventional sense but she was a powerhouse in her own right, a woman of excellence, someone you could not help but admire.

As we flipped through the pages of the book, he pointed to a picture and said, "One day this woman will be you."

At the time I was only seven or eight years old and did not understand what he meant. I didn't realize he was speaking over me and saw in me something I could not envision on my own.

I looked at him and said, "I'm a girl. I'll never be that old." He laughed.

The woman in question was Mother Theresa. In my home today there hangs a sign, a gift given to me by a woman I admire that quotes Mother Theresa. It reads:

"People are often unreasonable and self-centered. Forgive them anyway.

If you are kind, people may accuse you of ulterior motives. Be kind anyway.

If you are honest, people may cheat you. Be honest anyway.

If you find happiness, people may be jealous. Be happy anyway.

The good you do today may be forgotten tomorrow. Do good anyway.

Give the world the best you have and it may never be enough. Give your best anyway.

For you see, in the end, it is between you and God. It was never between you and them anyway."

Larry's murder was one of the most difficult times in my life. I felt cheated, angry, a pain that I can only describe as unbearable at times and completely lost. Larry was the person I called to keep me in line. He counseled me on my faith walk and scolded me when I needed it most. In life, you need to build genuine relationships where telling the truth, though it may sting, is what can be heard and discussed without anger or resentment. At the end of the day that friend, loved one will still love you and you them for pointing out your flaws.

For almost two years after Larry's death, I did not go to church outside of events for his anniversary and family events like christenings, weddings, etc. I had joined my husband's church after a very emotional experience during service one Sunday afternoon, but I still had a hole in my heart. For a brief period, my husband and I ran away to Florida thinking it would heal all the loss we had encountered since 2000, but it only made things worse. After just a year in Florida, we uprooted our family yet again and came home to New York.

One Sunday morning we went to the 11 a.m. service at the Cathedral. We were about 30 minutes late, and I couldn't find anything to wear as many of our things were still in boxes. So I threw on a velvet skirt and top that I pulled from the bottom of a box in my son's room. The kids were not cooperating with me that morning, and my husband couldn't find his black tie, yet again. We attempted to sneak into the back of the church quietly but with four children quietly never really ever happens.

As I went to sit down, Bishop Brown called me to come up to the altar. I thought to myself, *darn it... he caught me. Darn it that discernment.* My husband used to say he thought Bishop had his own private investigator because he not only preached about your situation but he went down your block, into your house and into your closets. We joked that Bishop was C.I.A.A (Covert Investigator Anointed Approved).

My hair was a mess, and I did not feel that beautiful that particular morning. When I finally made my way to the altar, Bishop walked down from the pulpit and joined me in the center of the "miracle aisle" as the church calls it and greeted me with a big teddy bear hug... his usual style. He then called his wife, Dr. Jasmine Brown, to come down from the altar and stand next to me. I wasn't sure what he was up to, but I was getting nervous.

He then proceeded to say these words, "Mother this is your daughter now. Daughter this is your mother now."

Those words struck me so hard, my eyes began to well up as if I was being cleansed internally.

Dr. Brown laid one hand on my stomach and the other behind my back and began to pray. I lifted my hands and my legs began to weaken. I could feel a fire in my stomach and tears advanced to weeping. From that day forward, the hole in my heart was now filled with the love of a new family. Dr. Brown became Mother Brown that day. Not only did I get a new spiritual father, but I also received a mother, which I never really had before.

Then, I also received a big brother in the person of Pastor Sylvester A. Brown and a whole host of stepmothers, sisters and brothers. Larry began my journey and he will always remain my daddy but the marathon he began with me as a child had now entered into the fifth hour and he passed the baton to my spiritual father, Bishop Sylvester O. Brown. I only pray that every person in this book will find the love and affirmation I received from my church family.

Women of Love

In 1979, a priest decided that he wanted to help a family that was adversely affected by the Vietnam War. He convinced his church's leadership and his congregation to align with him in this mission. He asked ten families to extend their homes and resources to this new family, my family, that was about to come to America. One very special woman, the mother of five, named Claire stood up without hesitation and offered to help. When we finally stepped onto American soil, Claire was named Godmother for all of us - my mother, my two sisters and me. Though we did not understand the purpose of the ceremony or why the young priest dressed in a gown was placing his hands on our heads with oil. We smiled and did as we were told.

The years came and went. Claire was firm and loving at the same time. When she babysat, she made us clean up our entire room before she would allow us to go out to play and the room had to pass inspection too. As the youngest, I called Claire – "Clairey". When I was about five years old, I wanted to get her a gift for Christmas so I found a used bottle of perfume my mother had on her dresser, filled it with water and gave it to her. She loved it! Later in her years, she shared many stories with me and the perfume incident was one of them but one of the things she cherished most was a note I had written to her while away at 4-H camp. The note had written on it, "*To know you is to love you.*" I don't recall writing the letter, but I definitely believed what I wrote.

Clairey's passing occurred while my family and I were in Florida. She was supposed to come with us that year, but she was low on funds, which prevented that from happening. I recall standing in the corner of the funeral home and just weeping. Fr. Larry was there to support me and he helped me get through her loss. He whipped away my tears and took my sister and I out to lunch after the funeral. We shared stories about Clairey, and the following day we spent the day together in Manhattan checking out the sites just like old times.

A year later, I learned how to cope but still felt a loss. After the death of my mother-in-law, two women phased into my life. I don't recall the exact moment when we became so close or the exact event, all I know is that these two women of love have taken and filled in their own way the loss of Clairey. One always seems to know when to call, she always has the right words of encouragement and wisdom at just the right time. She never ceases to pray and she wraps that same love around my entire family. It's almost if our families have merged into one. Her daughters are like my sisters. These are two of the only women I would trust with my children.

When my husband and I struggled silently to keep our family fed and maintain a roof over our heads, she was there. She never told anyone of our struggles. She never judged us or made us feel less important than others. She made sure our children had Christmas gifts under the tree and a feast on the table. This was just her nature. She is a petite woman in size but a giant women in love. One Sunday morning, Mother Johnson called me over to her when I poked my head into the church office.

She gave me a hug and said, "Hi, baby how are you?"

"I'm okay."

She grabbed my hand and placed her other hand over mine and said, "Do me a favor come see me after service."

"Okay."

After service, I asked my husband to get the kids in the car and pull the car around behind Mother Johnson's vehicle. I waited about 30 minutes for her to give out her hugs and kisses to the children, grown and little, of the church. She grabbed her jacket and waved for me to come on.

I followed her to her car, She unlocked the car and walked to the driver's side and shouted over the car, "Come on now, get in."

I did as I was told and waved my husband to follow us. When we arrived at her home, she flew the car door open as she turned off the key and said, "Let's go."

I looked at her strangely, what was she doing. The best way to describe Mother Johnson is to relate her to a bee that never stops and always has a purpose. She is always active. So, I followed her across the street and tried to keep up.

I tugged on her sleeve, "Mom, where are you taking me?"

"Oh, I'm sorry you know how Mother Johnson gets, this is my home. Come on, come on," she said as she pulled my arm by the wrist.

As she fumbled for her keys, I just stood there and looked around. Soon the door was open. "Come on in. Oh, I know I have it here somewhere," she mumbled.

"Have what, mom?" I asked.

Her home was as classy as she was and as beautiful. She began to look through a closet that was over packed and talked to herself.

"Yes, yes... it's here. I know it is. Here we go."

She pulled out a long denim jacket with purple fur as the inner lining with the price tag still attached. I had never shared with her that my youngest daughter did not have a new winter jacket.

She handed it to me and said, "Here you go, for my baby girl."

"Mom, it's beautiful but there are others at the church who need this more than us."

"But I want your daughter to have it."

"Are you sure?"

"Absolutely!" She looked at me and hugged me. "Love you all, praying for you."

I did all I could to hold my tears and hugged her back, "Love you mom."

She replied, "Love you more."

The second woman of love has known my husband since childhood. He was her son's protector in elementary school before he began a Golden Gloves boxer. They remained good friends throughout high school and into adulthood. She was at my wedding and celebrated with us at every major event in the lives of each of our children. When my mother-in-law passed in 2004 we began to talk and continue to talk to this day. Oh boy do we talk and talk and talk. She's quick to the punch and someone that truly lives to make others laugh. She treats our family like an extension of her own. She likes to chat and can be as slow as molasses, at times, but it's who she is. She'll give anyone a moment and I'm certain given the opportunity would be great at stand up comedy.

When I gave birth to my fourth child, she helped, not only me, but my husband. I went into labor about an hour before her only daughter. She lived seven hours away. She was sneaking phone calls on her cell phone while in my hospital room. During our pregnancies her husband teased about who will win the race. My due date was about a month and a half behind their daughter's.

As my labor became more intense and the doctors confirmed my son was in a breach position and that they could not delay the labor process any longer for the sake of both of our lives.

The doctor told my husband that if we waited any longer, both my life and the baby's life would be in danger and he may have to choose one over the other. She stood by him and placed her hand on his back, nodded and then held his hand.

He took a few minutes and said, "Save them both."

The doctor nodded and smiled with his mouth closed. Soon thereafter a nurse entered the room and had me sign a bunch of papers.

She prepared me for surgery and I was wheeled into the surgery room for prep.

The nurse asked, "Who will be accompanying her during the surgery?"

My husband took a step back and whispered, "I can't. I'll wait outside."

Felicia chimed in, "I'll do it. I need scrubs with ventilation she added. It's hot in here."

The nurse looked at her oddly since the temperature in the room was a cool 65 degrees. She quickly gave her some scrubs and Felicia asked for scissors to make her own ventilation. The nurse began to laugh. So, Felicia put her scrubs on backwards to create her own ventilation.

The nurse said, "You know you have your scrubs on backwards."

Felicia retorted, "It's my own V-neck design. You like it," as she struck a Vanna White pose. The nurse laughed as she left the room.

I was quickly wheeled into the surgery room and given an epidural. I began to cry as the nurse held my hand and assured me all would be okay.

I looked at her and said, "It's too early."

The nurse replied, "It will be okay."

Within about 30 seconds I could no longer feel my body from the waist down. I was lifted onto the surgery table and provided a special heated blanket. I was shivering as the room was an ice box. I heard the voices of about four doctors and in walked Felicia. The anesthesiologist directed her toward my head and instructed her to stay on that side of the screen and the doctors would remain on the other side. She was in heaven in the ice cold room.

In her usual style, she held my hand and began to tell jokes. As I chattered my teeth, I keep laughing and asked her to stop telling jokes because it hurt to laugh. She held my hand as the doctor poked around. I could feel the pressure of his hands as he searched for my son but no pain. Before long we heard a screech and then a banging against the glass window...and then a loud cheer from my husband.

The doctor announced, "It's a boy."

He laid a teddy-bear-sized little angel onto my chest for a brief moment and both Felicia and I began to cry. The baby was then intubated and quickly rushed to the Neonatal unit. I don't recall much thereafter except for receiving a kiss on the forehead from both Felicia and my husband.

She said, "You did good mommy." And then I vaguely remember them speaking in the corner, but soon drifted off.

This was one of the scariest moments in my life. My pregnancy had been tumultuous from the day we learned I was pregnant. When my husband couldn't handle the thought of possibly losing me or our newborn child, Felicia stood in and gave us the support and love we needed at the time. Quietly, I was yearning for my mother who could not be with me, but she was the next best thing. She kept me calm in the midst of the drama that surrounded me and my child's birth and she gave my husband the peace of mind he needed to get through that drama.

Best Friends Forever (BFF)

At the age of five, I met a young girl who looked nothing like me. She had pretty blond hair that was always in two ponytails, and I had jet black shoulder length hair with thick bangs. We quickly became friends but both of us remained individuals. Her name was Maureen but I called her Moe. She grew into a free spirited individual that I sometimes think she should have been a young adult in the 70's instead of a child. She liked to where tie dye designed clothes, hated to wear shoes and was a dedicated Grateful Dead follower. Just to demonstrate how much she loved the Grateful Dead, she sat vigil in her home when Jerry Garcia died. I never quite understood their music but when I went to visit with her I had to listen to it.

Moe was adventurous and not afraid to try new things, even if they could potentially be dangerous to her. She would still try just about anything once. As we entered into our teen years, our lives began to take very different paths. Moe's friends and my friends would not be caught dead in the same room. I loved R & B music, my favorite was Boys II Men, and wore preppy clothes from the GAP and Aerospostale. While in grammar school and throughout high school we signed all our notes to each other BFF (best friends forever). Knowing of some of Moe's choices - some potentially dangerous - I kept having a reoccurring dream that she would die before the age of 30. I prayed that this terrible dream was just my own internal fears and that this would not come true. She was a bridesmaid at my wedding and we were waiting for the time to celebrate her special day.

On Memorial Day weekend, my husband and I decided to do some furniture shopping for our new house in Florida. As we were walking around the display area of one particular furniture store my cell phone rang. It was my sister, who was in New York helping my parents sell their home.

"Hey, Happy Memorial Day," she shouted.

"Geesh, what are you so excited about?"

"Just glad to be alive," she replied.

"Okay?" I thought her comment was odd at the time.

"Listen, have you spoken with Maureen lately?" she asked.

"No, I haven't had a chance to call her and give her my new info. Why, what's up?" my sister almost never asked about Moe so I knew there was more to this question.

"Well, I don't know if this is true but there is a rumor going around that she died."

"Really, and who told you this, Mrs. Mancini? You need to stop gossiping. If she died, I'm certain her family would have called me. When did she supposedly die?" I asked quite annoyed.

"Well, the family's being really private about it. Mrs. Mancini says she thinks last month. Can you call to find out? They'll definitely tell you the truth."

"Are you crazy? I'm going to call her mom and ask if Moe's still alive. You've really lost it." I was becoming more and more agitated.

"I'll think about it. I gotta go. I'll call you later." I put the phone into my purse and walked toward the front of the store, sat down on the edge of a bed and stared out the window.

My husband walked over and said, "What's wrong?"

"My sister just called and said Moe's dead." I began to cry.

"Is it true?" he asked as he put his arm around me and my son jumped up behind us, "AJ cut it out," he shouted as he swatted him off me.

"I don't know but my heart is telling me that she's gone. What am I going to say to her mother? They're like family. Why wouldn't they call me so I could say goodbye?" I kept shaking my head.

My husband helped me to my feet and we left the store.

When we arrived at home he said, "You need to find out." He handed me the phone, "Call them and just act like you're giving an info update." So, I did.

When I returned home from church the following day, my husband was sitting in our office with his head down. He waved me to come into the office. I pushed into the VCR a copy of "Barney Blasts Off" and walked toward the office.

"Come in and close the door behind you." he said.

I began to get frantic, "What's wrong? What happened?"

"Just listen." he pressed the messages button on our answering machine.

Hi, ..umm I don't know how to say this, but it's Bobby. I picked up your call and didn't want mom to hear it. She's suffering so much right now... Maureen died last month and I am so sorry we didn't call you. It was so unexpected and we are all just trying to cope the best we can. Please know that Maureen loved you like a sister. You were a great friend to her over the years. Bye.

My husband caught me before I collapsed onto the couch. He wrapped his arm around me and held me for a while before I got up to go into our bedroom. He took the kids to the park so I could have my time. After they left, I sat up against the wall in my room and wept. I found an old picture of Moe and I just after we graduated from eighth grade. We sat back to back. She was wearing a tie dye tee-shirt, and I had on a white tee shirt and black blazer. Our hair was intertwined and she and a glow around her face. I smiled remembering that day. We were so excited about going to high school.

I called my pastor and he calmed me down. I began to pray for her family and our friends. I didn't have a BFF after that. No one could ever quite fill her shoes. Then I met my best friend Catherine. She was a young mother just like me at my church. Our daughter's were about the same age. One of the church mothers introduced us one evening after Sunshine Band rehearsal. Our first conversation was a bit awkward, but we exchanged numbers none the less.

She called me about a week later and said, "I don't want you to think I'm gay or anything, but I feel a real connection to you."

I felt the same. We spoke for about two hours.

About a week later, she brought her daughter over for a play date with my daughter. And as she prepared to leave we were standing in my foyer. On either side of my front door there were two long windows. We were talking about church leadership and she mentioned that she was having some difficulty figuring out her role.

I looked at the sunlight shining through the windows and said to her, "Remember what ever you decide to do... evangelize or be a youth leader that you are only a filter for those that come behind you to shine through. We are but servants and God's love and spirit should shine that much brighter through us."

She hugged me and said, "This is why I love having you as my friend."

Today, when we speak on the phone, our conversations last for hours. She moved back home to Tennessee.

We don't talk as often as we like, and the children keep us busy, but we always connect every few months or so. When our spirits are low, we have each other. When we need a little extra prayer power, we call on each other. When we succeed, we celebrate together, we laugh, laugh, and laugh. She is the Godmother of my youngest child, and though she is so many miles away, she is my BFF.

Not only do we have to balance time but we also need to balance emotions. We all carry many memories, hopes, wants, and hurts from our past. Loss of a loved one is one of the strongest hurts one can endure especially when it is sudden. Those that are taken from us earlier than expected are often the ones that stand out the most, the ones that have made the greatest impression to others.

Larry in so many ways lived up to his byline on Newsday after his death, "Saint on Earth," and Maureen lived life like no one I've ever known. She loved every minute and made each encounter with another person unforgettable. Her smile and silliness are what I miss most about her. Though Clairey led a full life and died in her late 70's, she never ceased to amaze me with her strength in spirit and personal desire to enjoy ever moment of her life. She made us understand the strength of family and the importance to always protect and love family no matter how stupid they may act. Loving another person does not mean becoming a stepping rug. It means you support them and allow them to go through difficult times so they can grow and mature. She watched me go through many events in my life but always loved me before, during and after the storm.

Chapter Six: Balancing the Beam

Balance is such a very important ingredient to a healthy, progressive and peaceful life. If you are a family of one or a family of six, caring for, planning for, protecting for, providing for them is no small feat. You learn how to become a master scheduler; you learn to wake up two hours earlier to make dinner in the morning so you can come home to a completed meal at 6:30 pm after a long day at the office; you learn to pack the school bags and briefcase the evening before (in most instances, at least); you learn to lay out your clothes or the options on your dresser the evening before; you learn to label all the leftovers so your family eats them; and you learn to pray for the ones you love daily. What you don't learn is balance. I only realized that I was out of balance last year on Christmas Day.

The Absent Mother/ Wife

I was walking around my living room with my robe on picking up wrapping paper and throwing it into the garbage pail. As I was making my way around the room, I noticed that my husband was staring at me.

It made me feel uncomfortable so I blurted out, "What are you looking at?"

My husband flinched, startled a bit. "Oh, just you."

"What about me? Do I have something in my teeth?" I began to pick at my teeth.

"No." he laughed.

"What then?"

"This is the first time in over six months that you have been home." he said.

"What the hell are you talking about? I've been home a lot. I'm here every night with you and the children. I even worked from home last week. " I huffed.

"You've physically been here, but you've been distracted. On the phone. On the computer. Trouble shooting a problem with a client or application. Researching for a project. Working, not home with us... We miss you. I miss you."

His words hit me hard and I began to cry. "Have I really been that involved in my work?"

"Worse." he smiled.

"I'm so sorry baby. I won't do that anymore. Family time is family time." I stopped what I was doing and hugged him and then the kids piled on top of the both of us. We laughed and then had a tickle war.

We live in an era of immediacy with every application on our Blackberry or I Phone, whichever addiction you own. I like Facebook just as much as the next person, but do I really need to log in five times a day or check how many posts have been added to my page more than once a day. Do I really need to or rather do people really care that I just landed in Denver on Twitter? If they are giving me the ride to my hotel they'd better.

Remote access does not mean constant access. It means if you need to check or work off site it's available to you. Unless your office is on fire, flooded, being robbed, or you're on the verge of losing a client then you do not need to get involved. You need to have faith in your co-workers that they will get the job done and you can relax and give all of yourself to those you love... time, mind and heart.

The Definition of NO

Kim was a giver. If she believed in something she gave of her time and money. She was a very talented marketing and communications professional with a middle management position. She was the co-director of her church's media ministry, Secretary of the National Association of Marketing Professionals, member at large of her college's alumni association, team mother of her daughter's soccer team, a board member of both the YMCA and the YWCA, and on the advisory committee of the Pick Em' Up Development Corporation. Needless to say, Kim was active. Not only did she serve in these capacities, but all of her appointments were hands on.

After six months, her rigorous self-induced schedule began to wear on her. She had caught the flu for the first time in five years while on a business trip in Detroit. She lost her voice during a trip in Texas and then had asthmatic bronchitis the first time in her life, which kept her home for a whole week where she had barely enough energy to eat. Her various organizations began to call on her and since they did not know she had over committed her time, pressed upon her the need to keep their needs and objectives as her prime focus.

The quality of her work began to diminish and she became sloppy, forgetting appointments and not responding to email within her usual 24 hour turn around time frame. Many of Kim's colleagues watched her unravel. Some were concerned while others enjoyed the show. One day her colleague who continuously attempted to compete with her, knocked on her door.

"Can I come in?" he inquired.

She waved him into her office as she finished a phone conversation. "Hey Martin. Can I help you?" she smiled.

"I'm writing a pitch and I have to insert a logic model. Do you know how to do that?"

Kim rolled her eyes in her mind and said, "Yes I do but no I can't help you."

Martin was puzzled. "What do you mean no? We are a team, remember."

"Martin you are the Director and intelligent enough to figure it out so figure it out." She got up from her chair and opened her office door. Martin jumped up and swiftly stammered out of her office.

Kim finally realized she had to learn to set limits. Whether you are an assistant or a C.E.O you must learn when and how to prioritize your time, whom you should spend time with and speak to and what projects are aligned to your end all goals. If this is not the case, simply don't do it. Kim was without a doubt sincere in her heart but unrealistic. If you must choose to be involved in activities outside of work and home ensure it is a cause or with people who will truly appreciate your sacrifice.

Married to the Computer

Darren was a committed and loving husband and father until he discovered the computer. Not only did he teach himself how to create websites but he also tried to teach himself how to repair the computer towers too. Mary had a storage house of seven computer towers in her foyer closet, not clothes, not shoes but computer towers. She had two black bags of computer parts that were pulled from the towers and various sprays and specialized cleaners. At first she thought Darren's new hobby was great. He was learning and staying out of her hair but then it became obsessive.

One all-nighter became a daily all-nighter. Darren still got up to go to work but he gained the new nickname of the yawner by his colleagues. Soon after the all-nighter's began during the day when he got home from work and after he ate his dinner, of course. Mary became accustomed to taking care of their two children by herself. She had a running joke that Darren was cheating on her with Dellia (DELL).

She sat and watched "Desperate House Wives" while he typed away on the computer in the den. Her agitation grew to anger and soon she locked him out of their bedroom but he just slept on the couch in the den. And then she locked him into the den and out of the rest of the house. He stood outside and banged on the door.

"Come on, let me in." he shouted.

"No, are you married to me or that stupid computer." Mary shouted from the second story window.

"Are you kidding me? You're jealous of a computer."

"Not jealous, you spend more time with that stupid machine than me or the kids."

"No, I don't. You're being ridiculous. Let me in my house." He began banging on the door again.

"Really? When was the last time we had sex?" she shouted.

Darren paused for a few minutes.

"Yup, you can't remember, can you. It's been that long."

"Our marriage is based on more than sex," he said smiling.

"You didn't get any points for that," she retorted.

"Come on, I'm hungry and its getting dark."

"Not until you promise to pay more attention to me and the kids and to leave Dellia alone or at least for a limited amount of time a day."

"Okay, I promise. Open the door."

"Pinky sware."

"Okay, pinky sware. Now, let me in!," he screamed.

Mary ran down the stairs and unlocked the door. She went to the living room to watch television.

"I'm going to start giving you attention right now." He ran behind her, picked her up and they went to their bedroom. Mary and Darren fell onto their bed in laughter.

Priorities are such an important part of character. Whether you make a seven figure salary or a five figure salary, remember what's most important – time with your family and friends. Machines and gizmos will always be there, but family may not. Don't look back and say only if because only if really means why didn't I? Take the time to relax and vacation, really vacation without technology, except for phones, of course, for emergencies, and enjoy the laughter of your wife, the playfulness of your children, and the peace of happiness.

Support and love can come from many places. Build a network of people around you that will be positive and cheer for you even when you don't feel like cheering for yourself. No man or woman is an island. We all need people, we need someone to lean on, someone we can trust with our hopes, fears and dreams, someone who will love us despite our flaws, someone who will carry us when we can not walk, and someone who cares for us intimately and personally. As the Hezekiah Walker song says, "I need you, I need you, we're all part of God's family... I need you to survive." We all have purpose but not all of us have discovered what that purpose is or how to live it out - that happens over time. If you are lucky enough to have one, maybe even more than one person that fits the description above, give them that same support and love in return and don't ever take them for granted.

In life, everyone must find and seek out balance. On the next page there is an exercise that can help you do just that.

Balance Sheet exercise:

1. Do you love yourself enough to forgive yourself? _____

    _____

    _____

2. Where does your joy emanate from – how others make you feel or

    from within? _____

    _____

    _____

3. Do you lead from the front or from behind? _____

    _____

4. If today was your last day on earth, could you honestly say you are

    a good person? _____

    _____

5. Materialism fills voids, what fills your empty spaces? _____

    _____

    _____

6. How do you inspire and encourage yourself? _____

    _____

    _____

7. Whom do you refer to as your mentors? _____

    _____

    _____

Vonekham Phanithavong-Guthrie

8. What are your three greatest personal accomplishments (non-work related)? _____

_____

_____

_____

_____

9. a) Do you love and respect your parents and elders? _____

_____

_____

b) If yes, how does your behavior reflect this? _____

_____

_____

Chapter Seven: A Time to Sow and a Time to Reap

In life there is a time to sow and a time to reap. We sow when we are in preparation to support something that is yet to come. You sow through prayer, through the physical act of saving money to gain interest for the purchase of a large item that you hope to own, and through investing your time into something or someone you see promise in. You can not reap unless you sow. Farmers must first plant, then water, and then, and only then, can they gather a harvest. Now, a harvest is not a given. There are many elements that can smother, injure and even kill your harvest before one single plant can even sprout.

Untapped Talent

Fashion was and is Jenni's passion. She spent years in school perfecting her craft. Many expected her to become a successful and accomplished designer. During her final internship, Jenni had a terrible allergic reaction to the many fabrics in the clothing factory and was unable to complete her required time in order to graduate. She became depressed and packed up her designing tools in a box that she placed in the back of her garage.

Over ten years passed, Jenni pursued other interests, but again illness got in the way. She became a mommy of two and found herself a single mother with limited resources. She had to move in with her parents and depend on their help for her daily needs. Jenni's depression got worse. Her sister, Melinda, prayed for her daily. Melinda knew that was the only help she could give her. Jenni needed to get up and survive on her own.

One day Melinda realized one of her dreams – to become a published author. The books were very popular and she in her own right became a role model for women in business. Melinda had the idea to create a clothing line as an additional source of revenue. She asked Jenni if she could design the clothes late one evening.

"Hey sis, I have a question for you." Melinda said.

"Yeah, what's up," Jenni mumbled as she chewed her last bite of food.

"Do you still have your sketch pads from when you were at F.I.T?"

"Yeah, why? I haven't touch that stuff in forever."

"I know, do you think you still have some creativity in you?"

"I guess." Jenni's voice softened. "Why?"

"You know how well folks have responded to the books I've written."

"Yes?" Jenni responded.

"Well, I decided to do a clothing line and think you are the talented designer I need to make this happen." Melinda smiled.

"Me, but … its been like forever since I touched a sketchpad. I don't know." Jenni's voice cracked.

"What are you talking about? You are so talented. This is your gift to the world. I know you can do this. If this works, you'll be able to take care of yourself and the kids."

Jenni began to cry, "I can't... I'm scared."

"Scared of what? I'm here to help you along the way. You've been sitting on this gift for too long." Melinda's voice got louder. "God doesn't give us gifts so they can lie dormant. What's the worse that can happen... no one buys the clothes."

"Yeah, but... I'm not like you. I don't think I still have it in me." Jenni retorted.

"You'll never know until you try. Just try? Please." Melinda pleaded. "For your baby sis."

"Okay, I'll try but what if I'm not good enough"

"You're good enough, actually you're great enough. Stop doubting your talents. I'll call you tomorrow to talk about this some more. Love you."

"Love you and ... thanks." Jenni hung up the phone.

Melinda found an opportunity where she could bless her sister, Jenni. She knew Jenni needed a push and support to live out her dreams and reap what she had invested so much time and dedication to many, many years ago. Privately, Jenni had been praying for an opportunity to return to her passion for fashion and God opened up that doorway through her sister's success.

Daddy's Home

Parents sacrifice and sow in order to protect their children from unseen dangers and to give them greater opportunities than they themselves had. Nicholas was an army general when his last daughter was born. He was so revered and trusted by his government that they tattooed the war plans on his back. They used this strategy to prevent their enemy from finding their strategy, but one of the high officials leaked the information after hours of torture. The government and Nicholas had to act fast so they aided him in his escape and advised his family that he had died in battle some days later. His youngest daughter was three months old when he left his family. He settled in France and prayed for his family's safety daily.

Twelve years later, a woman approached him one evening as he walked home from work.

"Hi, I'm sorry to bother you but are you Nicholas Phanithavong?"

"Yes." he replied.

The woman's voice began to squeak, "Your family is alive. You wife and three girls are in America."

Nicholas smiled and then tears came down from his eyes, "They're alive."

The woman smiled, "Yes. The girls are growing up so fast and your wife was able to escape."

He repeated, "They're alive."

"Come, let's go inside the hotel and talk some more." The woman took him by the hand and guided him into the hotel lobby.

He repeated again, "They're alive." He then hugged the woman and she began to cry. Some days later the woman set up a phone call between husband and wife. The call was filled with emotion, tears, laughter and joy. The church family that had brought Nicholas' family to America worked diligently to reunite the family. A year passed before all the paper work was approved and Nicholas was reunited with his family.

Nicholas left his family out of love... to protect them from Communist persecution. He knew that if his wife was aware he was alive, she would most certainly have been tortured like his friend for the information. So, he allowed the government to declare him dead. Though difficult, it was the only way. He thought about his family often and hoped for only good things for them. The reunion of the family was even more tearful and full of affection – an uncommon trait for a military general but a natural trait for a loving father.

An Unexpected Surprise

In 2003, I decided that I wanted to pursue my Master's in Public Administration. Initially, I began my studies at New York University, but after one semester I realized the commute was to much and that I needed a program that was more hands on and less theory based. After a year off, I enrolled in Long Island University on the C.W. Post campus. The program was for the working student and had classes on Saturday and Sunday. The professors were active and successful in their specialties. They even made me like statistics, one of the classes I barely survived through during my undergraduate studies. At the time, I had an old computer that kept freezing and it had all sorts of problems when I was writing my papers. In passing I shared this challenge with my dear friend, Felicia, and told her how I had to go to the school library to do my work.

One afternoon, Felicia called me to come by her house and said her husband had a surprise for me. Her husband, Robert, played a key role in my husband's upbringing even acting as his troop leader for the Boy Scouts. He always has something wise to share and knows a great deal about a lot. When I arrived to the house, Felicia told me to go down to the basement. Robert was in the shop area of the basement. He waved me to come in. On his work table he had a computer tower.

"Hey, what's up? What are you working on?" I asked.

"Just rehabbing an old computer."

"Oh, that's cool. Felicia said you had a surprise for me." I smiled a cheesy smile and he laughed.

"I am very impressed by you. You work so hard, you're a good wife to Matthew and take care of the kids. I know you are determined to get your masters degree and I believe you will be successful. I can't wait to read your first great novel." he paused.

I was overwhelmed by what he was saying. Robert never says a whole lot so when he speaks, you listen. He was a great success in his own career and he had counseled me in my career.

Vonekham Phanithavong-Guthrie

"So, I want to give this computer to you. I am customizing the features now. Promise me that you will not link the internet to this computer to avoid viruses. I hope you use this to write your first book. I believe in you." He then hugged me.

I held back my tears and thanked him. He carried the tower to my car, gave me a kiss on the cheek and went back in the house. I sat in my car and cried. This computer would allow me to work from home and spend more time with my family. It would allow me to live out my dreams and it was the tool that began the production of this book.

This blessing came from a very unexpected place. Even when you think you are not making an impression on another human being, you in fact are. Remember **you have true, genuine character when our behavior remains consistent whether or not eyes are watching**, whether or not we are being assessed through a performance evaluation, and whether or not we are receiving accolades for our actions.

Chapter Eight: With Thanksgiving and Humility

Success in life is what we all strive for. It is measured by different ways, by different people. Some view success as reaching a certain income level, others view it was acquiring a certain title within their company, while others measure it simply by your level of contentment in your life. I challenge you to find your own definition of success but remember to give thanksgiving when that success happens. What do I mean by Thanksgiving? Give thanks for the challenges you overcame and remember those that helped you along the way no matter how small the gesture was. Often it is the little acts of kindness that go the longest way.

Stay Together

There was a time in Shelly's marriage when she wasn't sure if her husband and she would remain together. They had suffered a series of deaths in their family and had both grown in their own ways. For a time they were separated and it was fairly certain this would be the end of their relationship. One Sunday, Shelly's mother-in-law asked if she could come to service with him for family and friends day. Shelly declined and went to her church instead but when she arrived in the parking lot her husband and his mother were waiting for her. So, she gave in and agreed to go to Love of God Church.

The service, as always, was beautiful. She received hugs and kisses from his mother's church family. Shelly's husband at the time looked a bit tattered. He wasn't clean shaven and his clothes were a little wrinkled. This was not the sharp dressed business man she knew. As they passed a crowd of people to leave the church, one of the church mother's called to them.

"Come here, you two."

She grabbed their hands, placed one on top of the other and then wrapped her hands around both of them and said, "Stay together. God has given you to each other as a gift." She smiled, let go of their hands and hugged them both.

No one knew of their separation or the marital struggles they were having so both were shocked by her statement. Plus, they had never heard this mother of the church, Mother Holmes, speak until that day. Later Shelly was advised by her husband's Godmother that if Mother Holmes says something you better listen.

About five years later, Shelly went to thank Mother Holmes for what she did and said, "That one statement reminded both my husband and I why we got married and that God was at the center of our union."

When Shelly thanked her she looked confused and said, "Baby, I don't recall saying that to you. It must have been the Holy Ghost. Well, praise be to God." Shelly smiled and hugged her.

Never miss the opportunity to acknowledge the kind acts of others toward you. As demonstrated in this story Mother Holmes did not even know that her one act had saved a marriage that was headed to divorce. You never know what another human being is suffering through and your smile, your hello may be all they need to get through the day, through the hour, through the moment. Kindness is not a sometime thing. It's an all time thing. Take a moment to say thank you.

Two Strikes

Dante was excited. He had just finished his last class for the summer accelerated program at school and was on schedule to graduate high school a semester early. He proved his father wrong, he was going to be something. Later that evening, Dante's boys picked him up to go to a house party in the neighborhood. Dante had been so focused on school that he hadn't really enjoyed summer break so he was ready to party. As the party winded down, and Dante gathered his boys to leave for the evening, his one friend, Curtis, was dancing with a beautiful blond bombshell. They were kissing in the corner when another young man with ash brown hair pulled the girl away by the arm and began cussing Curtis out.

Dante shouted, "Curtis, let's be out!"

Curtis turned to the girl – a bit tipsy – and said, "You can have her, we were just playin' bro," as he stumbled to his friends.

On the drive back home the boys were laughing until a white Corvette sped up along side them and cut them off. The passenger side window of the Corvette opened and the same young man with the ash brown hair stuck out his hand and put up his middle finger.

Then he shouted, "Suckers!!!"

Dante's friend, Jevon, was driving. He sped the car up and chased the Corvette for about two miles. Curtis and the other two boys in the car were getting hyped up and ready to fight. Dante sat there and played along, but he really just wanted to get home.

He kept saying, "Man forget them, they're punks. Let's be out!" hoping they'd let this go.

But they didn't, and before long the Corvette stopped and the boys jumped out of the car to fight. Dante held back until he saw his friend they called Tiny, the baby of the group, getting beat on by two other guys. So, he joined the fight to help his friend. Little did he know that Jevon had an unloaded gun and foolishly held the gun to the boy with ash brown hair and told him to give him all of his money.

Soon the fight was over, and the boys jumped into the car. It was then that Dante saw the gun. "What the hell did you just do?" Dante shouted.

"We got to get rid of this gun!" Jevon responded.

They took the gun to a young lady's house. They were all friends with her and then headed home. Just before they were about to approach Dante's cul-de-sac, cops pulled the car over and arrested the boys. All five boys were put into jail that night as the boy in the ash blonde hair shouted, "Dad, that's them."

Barbara's phone rang at 2 a.m. that morning. She was still groggy, but picked up the phone. Her sister, Katherine, was on the line, frantic. "They took Dante to jail... they took Dante to jail. What do I do? I need you sis."

Barbara took a few minutes to process what she was hearing. "What? Calm down and tell me what happened?"

When Katherine finally finished, Barbara was able to better think of how she could help. "OK, let me call some of my friends down there to find out what he's being charged with and find someone to check on him in jail. I'll get out there as soon as I can."

The next morning Barbara made a number of calls to her friends in Tennessee. She found out the seriousness of the charge and first began to pray and then began to strategize on how to help her nephew, Dante. He was held in juvenile detention until the charges were solidified and the judge allowed for Dante to be charged as an adult since his 18th birthday was soon approaching. Dante was then removed from juvi and sent to a maximum secure prison with adult offenders. Barbara booked her flight as soon as she learned of the change and knew she had to be in the state to make some things happen. She prayed some more and then planned another strategy. A week later she arrived in Tennessee.

Katherine in tears hugged her sister and said, "Dante's been asking about you. He needs you. I need you sis, I don't know what to do."

That evening they went to the jail for a visit. Since he was in an adult maximum facility, the visit was only via camera and for a limited 30 minutes. When they arrived at the visitors' site, the sign read "no items can be brought into the visitors chambers." Barbara showed her driver's license and then signed in with her Bible in hand. The guard looked at her, smiled, and then looked the other way. She went and sat by her sister on the metal benches outside of the visiting area. Before long, the announcement was made that visitors could now enter into the building.

Each station was equipped with a small box, cubicle like, a small 19-inch television screen and a yellow telephone. Dante appeared on the screen. His left eye was swollen. Katherine picked up the phone.

"Hi Dante, look who came to see you." She pulled Barbara closer to her and handed her the phone.

"Hey, baby boy. What are you doing in there?"

Dante turned his head and began to cry. "I'm sorry auntie. I didn't want you to ever see me like this. They beat on me everyday."

Barbara pretended to cough and turned her head, "Excuse me a minute baby." She handed the phone back to Katherine. She wiped her tears and regained her composure. She opened the Bible to the Lord's Prayer. Katherine rubbed her back and then handed Barbara back the phone.

"OK, well let's say a quick prayer before the session ends." Barbara read the Bible and held Katherine's hand. Dante bowed his head.

"OK, auntie I've been praying everyday. I don't think God hears me though."

"You keep praying…he hears you…and I'll keep praying. I love you, and I'll do what I can to save you from this." The screen went black.

Two weeks later, the lawyer Barbara had helped Katherine to secure was able to get Dante out of jail, but he was on house arrest. The judged approved for him to go to school, but he was not allowed to participate in any extracurricular activity.

Until then, Dante and his father were able to live together with minimal incident. But now that Dante was forced to be in the home. Old issues surfaced and tempers flared daily until one day when Dante had to get out of the house and that one day became that one night. This time, Dante was in a car with his friends and they were pulled over for a routine traffic violation when the officer noticed the bracelet on Dante's foot. He was immediately arrested and returned to jail. After the officers searched the car, they found two nickel bags of weed, which did not help Dante's case.

He was held in the adult maximum prison for over two months. The judge and the District Attorney wanted to make an example of him and were pushing for him to receive the max of 15 years to life for battery, robbery with the intent to injure. The charges continued to grow with every court date. As Dante prepared for his sentencing, Katherine called Barbara again in a panic. Barbara was angry with Dante, she had told him that he was only getting a second chance because of God's grace and not to forget that.

"B – What do I do? They're going to put him away. The lawyer's not helping."

Barbara prayed and said, "Ask the judge and the D.A. if they would allow for a private meeting in his chambers. I'll write what you need to say, just read it."

The request was permitted and the following week a private meeting was held. Dante gave his plea for leniency and then Katherine read the letter. The judge and the D.A. were so moved that they entered into private counsel. The following day sentencing commenced. Dante was given four years probation with the understanding that if he did not completely follow the orders he would be back in jail, and the judge would not be lenient next time.

Katherine called Barbara overjoyed, "He's coming home the week before Thanksgiving. Thank you sis."

"Don't thank me, thank God," she replied.

Some weeks later, Barbara received a phone call at 2 a.m. in the morning. She answered the phone, still groggy, and it was Dante. He was out of breath and his voice was shaking.

"What's wrong, what happened?" Barbara shouted.

"Nothing. I just wanted to tell you that I love you and thank you for praying with me and for me."

Barbara began to cry, "I love you...that's what you do when you love someone. Now, be humble in your second chance and do the right thing. Don't test God again because next time he may not answer. Love you."

"Love you." he replied and hung up the phone.

Student Speaker

Every year Columbia University hosts a very special reception to thank those who support scholarships to its students. This annual event brings together scholars and benefactors to provide them the opportunity to meet face to face. I was a senior and this would be my last reception. Over the two years that I spent at Columbia University, School of General Studies, I grew very close to my benefactor and to this day we remain good friends. The Dean decided that he wanted to do something different, so two days before the event, he asked me to say a few words that evening.

I went home that evening and thought about what I would say to this group of high net worth folks and my fellow students, many, of which, were my friends. I wrote four versions of a speech I never read and as I was looking through old pictures with my 5-year-old daughter, Destiny, she stopped my hand.

"Mommy, why are you dressed like that?"

She was referring to my graduation picture from Nassau Community College.

"That's when you have a party because you did something really good." I replied.

"Oh, so you're a winner," Destiny shouted as she clapped her hands.

I thought about what she said after I tucked her in for the night and read her "Brown Bear, Brown Bear," yet again and jotted down the speech that I ultimately ended up giving at the reception.

The evening of the reception was beautiful. It was a cool 65 degrees in the air. Excitement and anticipation were building up as the evening progressed in Lerner Hall that night. I greeted my benefactor with a hug and kiss on the cheek. Many of the other students she had blessed were anxiously waiting to speak with her at her table so I stepped aside to allow them time.

The benefactor in her usual way, pulled me to the side and said, "What a lovely event, I hear you're speaking tonight."

I smiled, "Yes, I wanted to mention how much you've supported me not only financially but as a friend."

"No, no please. I, the family does this out of love not for recognition." she whispered.

"OK," I knew exactly how I would still give her recognition without having to call her out of the crowd.

Throughout the course of the night, I keep looking around the room for my husband. As the time drew near for me to speak, we had Columbia's security looking for him. He had called me an hour earlier, and I knew he was on his way. Something didn't feel right.

Dean Awn approached the podium, quickly cleared his throat and said, "Good Evening and thank you to all of you for coming this evening. Each year we come together to celebrate education. Those that are receiving it and those that make it possible for students with great potential but limited financial means to attend and study at this great institution. We have decided to change the format of this evening's presentations and allow one of our star GS students, now in her senior year, to speak about her experience at GS. Please join me in welcoming to the podium...Vonekham Guthrie."

The room was at a stand still, my husband still nowhere in sight. I took a deep breath. The Dean of Students helped me to the podium and smiled. My heart began to race knowing that my words would impact those students that were yet on scholarship and whether or not their benefactors would make larger contributions in the year to come. I was blessed with a full scholarship while the rest of my college mates were only receiving ten or fifteen thousand dollars, which only scratched the surface of the cost to attend Columbia.

I stood straight up, shoulders back smiled and said, "Thank you Dean Awn for your kind introduction. First let me say, good evening to the esteemed benefactors, university administrators, friends and colleagues. I am humbled to have been selected to speak with you today. As I prepared for this evening, I thought about what GS meant to me, my family and to my fellow students. I thought of the rigor of our studies, the endless hours of reading, writing, reading and then studying and then studying some more. I thought of how difficult and a bit frightening it was to return to college after having taken a break from formal education. I thought about a very special person who I now not only refer to as my benefactor but as my friend."

My benefactor stood just to my right and I looked a her at that moment - smiled, she smiled back and gently nodded my head. "I won't be before you long but wanted to share a quick story with you that helped me to realize what this experience has meant to me. In my usual way, I was reading an assignment for school, Shakespeare's "Much Ado About Nothing," as part of my 5-year-old's bedtime story. As a mother of two small children, I had to find unique ways to get schoolwork into my otherwise hectic day. She laughed at the old English language and referred to it as funny words. After finishing reading, my daughter asked to look at a photo album that I had left on her dresser. I had intended to look through it after she fell asleep and actually get ten minutes to organize the pictures. I grabbed the album and we began flipping through the pages. We arrived at a picture of my graduation from Nassau Community College. She pointed to what I was wearing and asked why I was dressed like that. I explained that when you study real hard you get to wear a pretty cap and gold sashes. She responded, "Mommy... You're a Winner" and began to clap. It was then that I realized what GS had given me. Every person in this room is a winner, not because you are now an Ivy Leaguer but because you invested the time to invest in yourself and make the journey back to college despite the challenges that were in your pathway. I salute every benefactor for believing in education and taking the time to make a difference and I celebrate each and everyone of my classmates. Continue to work hard, stay focused and remember to count your blessings...I know I will. Thanks for your time and attentiveness. I will now give the podium back to our wonderful Dean, Dean Peter Awn."

Dean Awn gave me a hug, grabbed my hand and mouthed great job. As I stepped down, I was surrounded by cheering and clapping and then a sea of people started forming around me. My husband made his way through the crowd and gave me a big hug and kiss.

He whispered in my ear, "I'm so proud of you. This is your moment."

I was overwhelmed by the attention. Some benefactors asked if I'd consider running for political office and offered to finance me. Others shook my hand and said thank you for reminding them why they give each year.

My benefactor simply hugged me and said, "Superwoman has now taken flight, good job. Proud of you."

Superwoman was a nickname she had given to me after she read my college application and agreed with the administration of GS that I needed to be the first Program for Academic Leadership and Service, better known as PALS, scholarship a year early than it was scheduled to launch.

Humility is an honorable attribute. It reminds us that we are not to over praise ourselves because then we lose sight of the reason we began a project or mission in the first place. When you reach a certain level of success, many people will try to place you up on a pedestal and it's fine for them to admire you but not to worship you. Worship is reserved for only one person and that is God. My benefactor is a great example of humility. She and her family have provided many, many young adults the ability to go to college simply because they believe in education. Non-profit organizations follow the same principle. They do the hard work many do not want to do... educating the impoverished, feeding the broken with food literally and emotionally, clothing the helpless and so much more simply because they believe in it. Learn to thank others for their compliments without stroking your own ego. A bloated ego can lead to many disastrous results and poor decision-making.

Humility can be difficult at times. When you are adored and revered by others it can easily give you a misguided notion that you are larger than life. When in fact you are the same person that was awkward and unsure of yourself in middle school, just a more developed version with new strategies to cover up your timid nature. Ego is another area where people become deluded in believing that their presence on this world out shines that of others. In reality, you get dressed just like everyone else. The only difference is you have less privacy and more eyes are watching you.

Many people dream of fame and stardom, but what is the price of that level of exposure? Your life is no longer your own. Much is sacrificed and sometimes lost. You become a walking breathing public relations pitch. If you notice those celebrities whose careers span over time are more grounded and often live their private life in private. They try to at least. They realize that there is a time and a place to be fabulous and photographed and then there is a time and place to be the everyday regular person that runs his or her own errands, goes food shopping and drops their children off to school. If you seek out the spotlight, the spotlight may fall on you.

No matter where life takes you remain humble. Don't allow your success to change you or worse control you. Remember those that supported you along the way and recognize their role in making you who you are. Your parents, your friends, your minister, rabbi or monk, your mentor...they all have contributed in developing all the characteristics that have given you the ability to stand taller, aspire higher and become a success. As the old adage says, *We Stand on the Shoulders of those that have Come before us.* Never forget that and you will be a happier, more successful human being.

As in the case of young Dante, he learned in a tough love way how to say thank you. Unfortunately, sometimes tragedy must strike before we can see the many blessings that surround us. Joy does not appear when you earn seven figures, though you can buy beautiful and ornate things. Joy comes from appreciating what you already have and realizing that you are already blessed. We all want to be appreciated and in management courses you learn that employees crave affirmation and recognition from their superiors. Salary increases are good too, but there is nothing like hearing your supervisor say, "Good Work" to you. Thank you goes a long way. It is one of the staple principles of the business I am in – non-profit fund raising and development – we build procedures and programs around saying thank you to our donors... to those that support us. As my pastor says time and time again, you support what you love. Take time everyday to say thank you and mean it!